# Communication,
# Curriculum
# and Classroom
# Practice

# Communication, Curriculum and Classroom Practice

CLARE LATHAM AND ANN MILES

The Redway School

**David Fulton Publishers**

London

David Fulton Publishers Ltd
Ormond House, 26–27 Boswell Street, London WC1N 3JZ

www.fultonpublishers.co.uk

First published in Great Britain by David Fulton Publishers 2001

*British Library Cataloguing in Publication Data*
A catalogue record for this book is available from the British Library.

ISBN 1–85346–732-4

Typeset by Book Production Services, London
Printed in Great Britain by Bell & Bain Ltd, Glasgow.

# Contents

## Dedication

This book is dedicated to the children and
their carers at The Redway School
who continue to guide our teaching

# Foreword

For many years now, Clare Latham and Ann Miles have been taking research in education and speech and language therapy and making it accessible to fellow practitioners working with children and young people with severe and profound learning disabilities.

In their writing, and in their practice, they have provided an exemplary model of collaborative working between a teacher and a speech and language therapist.

It should not surprise us, then, to find Latham and Miles at the forefront of initiatives for implementing National Curriculum English (Communication and Literacy) for students below Level One. *Communication, Curriculum and Classroom Practice*, however, goes further than this. It offers a well substantiated and integrated approach, taking us from background theory, to assessment through to a framework for a complete scheme of work for English, incorporating the latest QCA guidelines for students with significantly below age-related expectations, mapping p-levels onto descriptors and objectives.

This book takes an explicitly developmental framework. This is not without problems. We cannot always assume that learners, especially older learners, with severe and profound learning disabilities will follow typical developmental routes. However, it does give education and therapy staff a clear framework from which to work. In the case of Latham and Miles' framework, it also has the virtue of giving parallel stages of 'thinking skills'.

For each of the four bands of development, a cycle of assessment, planning and sample lesson plans is provided. This could sound worryingly like a 'cookbook' of recipes for communication development, but, in general, it is concepts and examples that the reader is offered; the rest depends on individual teachers' creativity.

Progress in the development and use of language and communication is central to the life chances of young people with severe and profound learning disabilities. This puts great pressure on teachers, therapists and, of course, the young people themselves and their parents. We are all looking for the best approaches to teaching and therapy, the optimal contexts and the latest techniques. Latham and

Miles have kept in mind the long-term needs of the young people they work with, as well as their current developmental levels. In doing this, they have made the teaching of communication and, particularly, literacy, relevant and meaningful to children with severe impairments.

Whether we accept a developmental model or not, the incremental nature of learning to communicate cannot be denied. This sense of a cumulative skill comes across strongly, with ideas for subsequent bands developing existing skills and adding new ones over time. This aspect is particularly well demonstrated in the way that the teaching of literacy builds up from aesthetic literacy through functional literacy to formal literacy. Supporting this, is the use of Nicola Grove's work on early literacy and her perhaps better known writing with Keith Park (e.g. *Odyssey Now* and *Macbeth*). For learners at more advanced levels, there are challenging ideas for developing children's criticality as consumers of written fiction, TV and video.

In this book, teachers and speech and language therapists will find few wheels re-invented. Instead, Latham and Miles have drawn on their own professional experience at the Redway School and a thorough knowledge of published research. Into their framework they have successfully incorporated approaches such as Intensive Interaction, Special Times and objects of reference.

Of course, no book covers everything. Ideas for working with children who have additional impairments such as severe physical impairments requiring the use of Augmentative or Alternative Communication, those with hearing and visual impairments and autism, whilst included, are brief. However, the reference list provides plenty of scope for further reading in these, and other, areas.

The last fifteen years have witnessed a major change towards seeing all students, irrespective of their disabilities, as communicators. This book will contribute to taking that change a step further, towards the recognition that all students have the right to literacy.

*Juliet Goldbart*
*Manchester Metropolitan University*
*September 2000*

# Acknowledgements

Our thanks go to all the teachers at the Redway School, first for putting up with us and secondly, for proving to be such valuable critics in trialling the English Scheme of Work.

Special thanks to:

Judith Gale for her work on medium-term plans.

Ruth Jay for contributing her experience with PMLD students and in writing lesson plans.

Sue Rowley and Nicki Sigston for the social sight vocabulary.

Bernadette Shepherd for her creative work with sensory stories.

Jan Sidall for developing a coherent framework for objects of reference.

Julia Sims for contributing her understanding of Autistic Spectrum Disorders and for working on the objects of reference framework.

And the rest of the Redway staff for showing us that English can be such fun.

Mary Smith, the Director of Speech and Language Therapy for the Milton Keynes Primary Health Care Trust who gave us her active support and encouragement.

Finally, Richard Fraser, Head of the Redway School, who facilitated the writing of the book through his unwavering support for the concepts of a developmental curriculum and integrated working practices. His major contributions have included: providing information, stimulating debate and making us get on with it!

# Preface

As a teacher and a speech and language therapist, working with children who have severe and profound learning difficulties, we needed a curriculum which met the developmental needs of the children and enabled our two professions to work together in addressing educational issues and individual needs.

With this in view, we worked with the teachers at the Redway School, to develop a curriculum which could be taught within the classroom and meet both IEP and therapy objectives. The resulting English Scheme of Work, incorporated in *Communication, Curriculum and Classroom Practice*, has been successfully taught at the Redway School since September 1999.

This book aims to be a practical resource for both assessment and teaching. Its communication and cognitive framework reflects recent theories of child development. These inform the English Scheme of Work which focuses on the communication and literacy needs of developmentally young children.

The Scheme of Work includes the Qualifications and Curriculum Authority's pre-level one indicators – the P. Scales (DfEE 1998) within the Scheme of Work objectives, thus linking national indicators with the work carried out in the classroom.

Each band of the Scheme of Work has appropriate teaching and learning styles, guidelines for children with additional needs, suggested activities, sample lesson plans and a detailed assessment (a revision of the Redway School Communication Assessment).

It has been our experience at the Redway School that using a developmental approach to the curriculum has placed communication at the core of our teaching.

**Note**

The authors use 'he' as the neuter pronoun for the child, merely to keep the book uncomplicated.

*Chapter 1*

# The framework

In 1997 we published a communication assessment framework in which the first few years of early development were subdivided into four bands (Latham & Miles 1997). As we used the assessment, it became increasingly apparent that although each band was focused on communication development, there were clear links to cognitive development. This implied that the learning style which was most appropriate for communication skills was also right for developing cognition. We were aware of the debate concerning the link between communication and cognition and decided to explore this idea further.

The result was a framework (see Figure 1.1) which can be used as a foundation for both curriculum planning and classroom practice. The framework is deliberately kept as simple as possible, only the key features of each developmental level are included. This allows all the adults involved with children at early developmental levels to remember and apply it in practice.

The framework is designed to be a foundation for curriculum development, allowing schools to continue to be creative but to always ensure that the curriculum is appropriate for children at each developmental level. In the classroom, the framework reminds teachers and others of the teaching styles and interactive techniques which are most effective.

Using the framework throughout the school has ensured a consistency of teaching style, content and expectations.

*Description of the communication and cognition framework*

The framework charts functional communication and cognitive development through the early years. Four key stages (bands one to four) are identified and the essential elements of communication and cognition are highlighted at each band. The pre-level one indicators as described by the Qualifications and Curriculum Authority (QCA 1998) are linked to each band, for example band one links to P1, P2 and P3.

The first column looks at the key communicative functions used by children at each band as described by sociolinguistic theories of language development.

| Pre-level 1 indicators QCA | BAND ONE – PRE-INTENTIONAL Developmental language 0–5 months | | | |
|---|---|---|---|---|
| | COMMUNICATION FUNCTIONS | METHOD OF COMMUNICATION | DEVELOPMENT OF THINKING SKILLS | SUCCESSFUL COMMUNICATION REQUIRES: |
| P1 <br><br> P2 | Expresses: likes, dislikes, wants, understanding of familiar and unfamiliar. | The child expresses himself through: crying, stilling, smiling and vocalising. | Engages in sensory activities, relates to people or objects, explores objects by mouthing or banging, needs time to engage in non-routine activities. | An adult to respond and interpret behaviours. |
| | BAND ONE – INTENTIONAL Developmental language 5–9 months | | | |
| | COMMUNICATION FUNCTIONS | METHOD OF COMMUNICATION | DEVELOPMENT OF THINKING SKILLS | SUCCESSFUL COMMUNICATION REQUIRES: |
| P3 | Expresses: gains attention, requests, greets, gives information, responds by indicating yes or no. Understanding is related to routines. | The child expresses himself through vocalising, facial expression, pointing and gestures. | People and object play is integrated, explores the function of objects, combines objects. Uses everyday objects in play. | An adult to respond to the child's attempts to communicate and join in with turn-taking activities. |
| | BAND TWO – Developmental language 9–18 months | | | |
| | COMMUNICATION FUNCTIONS | METHOD OF COMMUNICATION | DEVELOPMENT OF THINKING SKILLS | SUCCESSFUL COMMUNICATION REQUIRES: |
| P4 | Requests more, actions and help, asks for the names of objects and people, attempts to say names, indicates own belongings, indicates that things have gone or finished, indicates where things should go, describes qualities e.g. 'YUK'. | Expresses through a combination of methods such as gesture, vocalising and using objects, leading to using the formal system of signs and words. | Learns through own activity, combines objects purposefully, sorting in play, simple pretend play, e.g. with dolls. | An adult to play, respond and comment on the game. |
| | BAND THREE – Developmental language 18–36 months | | | |
| | COMMUNICATION FUNCTIONS | METHOD OF COMMUNICATION | DEVELOPMENT OF THINKING SKILLS | SUCCESSFUL COMMUNICATION REQUIRES: |
| P5 <br><br> P6 | Socialises, gives information, describes, directs questions 'who' 'what' and 'where', repairs misunderstandings, understands and expresses in short sentences. | Uses words, signs and symbols in short sentences and phrases, e.g. 'Daddy go work'. | Sequences ideas in play, basic understanding of size, colour, number and position, needs to relate to here and now. | An adult to clarify misunderstandings, answer questions and make communication fun and rewarding. |
| | BAND FOUR – Developmental language 3–5 years | | | |
| | COMMUNICATION AND THINKING SKILLS | METHOD OF COMMUNICATION | | SUCCESSFUL COMMUNICATION REQUIRES: |
| P7 <br><br> P8 | Understands and expresses: reasons and predictions, plans activities, negotiates, questions to find out information, understands abstract ideas and language out of context, early numbers and alphabet skills. | Uses complex sentences containing joining words such as 'and', 'because'. | | An adult as an active listener to share ideas, clarify meanings and explain. |

**Figure 1.1** Communication and Cognition Framework

The second column lists the most common methods of communication used at each band charting the development from informal language systems such as crying and stilling through to the formal language of speech or signs.

The column entitled 'thinking skills' aims to show the key features of cognitive development at each band. This column is based on the work of Piaget (1952), and Uzgiris and Hunt (1975) as summarised by Coupe and Goldbart (1998).

Last, the fourth column incorporates Bruner's theories of the need for a communicative partner and states clearly what the adult must do to enable the child to learn and develop (Bruner 1975).

## Band one

Band one, the preverbal stage, is subdivided into Pre-intentional and Intentional communicators.

At the earliest level of pre-intentional communication the adult is required to interpret the child's behaviours and respond accordingly. An adult who knows the child well is usually able to interpret the following meanings: like, dislike, wants, rejects and responses to the familiar and unfamiliar.

Typical behaviours at this level are crying, stilling, smiling and vocalising. Many children with profound learning difficulties have complex and inconsistent means of expressing themselves, requiring careful observation and responses from the adult.

Cognitive development at this level enables the child to receive most stimulus from sensory experiences, i.e. kinaesthetic (movement), auditory, visual, taste, smell and touch. The most successful classroom activities involve using one or more of these senses. The child may enjoy engaging with an object, exploring it by simple means such as mouthing or banging.

Children will usually enjoy interaction with one other person, e.g. games involving eye contact or turn taking without objects. They are not able to interact with both a person and an object, i.e. they cannot yet 'share attention'.

Children progress to become intentional communicators, this means they refer purposefully to a communicative partner. An example is the child reaching up to a drink or toy but looking and vocalising at the teacher to request the object.

At this level they are able to express a wider range of meanings such as trying to gain attention to themselves, requesting objects or games, greeting familiar people and giving information (perhaps by showing their biscuit to the visitor). As children progress through this band they are able to indicate 'yes' or 'no'.

Children use a range of behaviours to express themselves which include vocalising, pointing, facial expression and other gestures.

Cognitive development focuses on exploring and understanding the use of a range of objects. Children begin to explore the function of objects, for example, pretending to drink from a cup they know is empty. They experiment with combining objects such as dropping objects into a container and they can share attention by playing with both a toy and an adult, for example taking turns to bang a drum.

The adult's role is to become the communicative partner, enabling the child to practice and refine their attempts at early communication. Turn-taking games both with and without toys are one of the essential elements of communication development at this level.

## Band two

As children become more adept at combining objects and involving adults in their play, they become highly active learners. Band two covers this period, where children progress from intentional communication, using a variety of methods until they have a vocabulary of about 50 words or signs.

The band is referred to as 'First Meanings' because the first communications are not clear words but ideas or meanings which the child wishes to communicate. For example, asking for 'more' dinner by pointing first to the serving dish and then to their own plate and vocalising at the adult.

Different authors identify a variety of first meanings; however Coupe O'Kane and Goldbart (1998) compiled a list of ten for children with learning difficulties. These include communications such as requesting 'more' (recurrence), indicating where objects or people should be placed (location) and informing others that objects have disappeared (disappearance).

First meanings are usually communicated initially through facial expression and body language. The child progresses to using a consistent gesture and vocalisation and finally a clear word or sign. It is a characteristic of this level that children are very individual about how they communicate and in what they wish to say.

Able-bodied children are very active and develop their cognitive skills through their own physical experiences. This involves single element role play with dolls and household items. They combine objects purposefully, using basic construction materials and a variety of toys such as pegboards and dough. Please see chapter 8 for a suggested list of materials. Categorisation skills develop through this active play as children begin to sort their toys. At first they may put all the dough in one saucepan and the beads in another. Later they put the red cup on the red plate and the green cup on the green plate.

The adult's role is to be a playful partner, providing appropriate materials, responding to the child and modelling formal language systems by commenting on the play.

## Band three

The dominant feature of this band is the ability to sequence ideas both in play and in communication.

Children use formal communication systems (signs, words or symbols – possibly a combination) to produce simple sentences or phrases, initially of two words, then as they acquire confidence, of three, four and more words. They extend the functions for which they use language to include some questions and descriptives. Children are able to understand short sentences containing key words.

As children begin to use longer phrases, articulation problems may become apparent and inhibit both communication and cognitive development. Children need to use and experiment with the meaning of new words and concepts. It is for this reason that Alternative and Augmentative Communication systems such as Voice Output Communication Aids, symbol communication books and sign systems may become crucial to the child's development.

Cognitive skills develop in parallel with these new linguistic skills. Lowe (1975) found that children began to link sequences of events in pretend play just before they began to link ideas in language. Children enjoy play with miniatures such as doll's houses, cars, farms and so on, often using simple language to describe their actions. An understanding of basic concrete concepts develops at this stage. This may include colours, size (big and small), prepositions(in front and behind) and adjectives (hot and cold). It is essential to remember that band three children find it very difficult to deal with any abstract concepts such as reasoning, or any ideas beyond the immediate environment. The most successful activities relate to concrete ideas which the children can experience at the time. Thus 'news time' is more effective if the children bring an object from home to help them to recall the significant event of the weekend, e.g. a brochure from the theme park visit.

The adult as a communicative partner has a role which includes clarifying word meanings and helping the child deal with the frequent misunderstandings which occur. More important, though, is making communication fun and rewarding, motivating the child to continue to communicate more information in more effective ways.

## Band four

At this developmental level, communicative and cognitive skills become interwoven. The child has developed sufficient language skills to use them to support learning. Children can understand language out of context and begin to deal with abstract ideas.

New language and cognitive abilities mean that the child can begin to use and understand reasoning, they can draw together several pieces of information to make predictions of what may happen in the future. Questions are used to find out information, for example, 'How does the television work?' A different set of questions dealing with complex ideas come into use – 'when', 'why', 'how'. As they begin to understand abstract concepts such as time, children can begin to plan future events and evaluate past experiences.

Language skills should have developed to include a vocabulary of several thousand words which are incorporated into complex sentences with various parts.

The formal language systems may involve Voice Output Communication Aids (VOCA), a device which can contain several thousand words is necessary for children at this cognitive level, a signing system which meets the needs of communicating abstract ideas, or a symbol system which can be used to link ideas. Developing and learning these alternative systems is challenging but necessary if children are to use their cognitive skills to the full.

The adult's role is to become an active listener, helping children to clarify their ideas and encouraging the thinking skills. This is the time for teachers to begin to use cognitively challenging questions such as 'what might happen next?' and 'why did he behave like that?'

# Chapter 2

# Theoretical background and the development of functional language

Until the 1970s, developing children's language was dominated by two main theories. Skinner's behaviourist theory (Skinner 1957) suggests that language is learnt in response to a stimulus that gives a pleasant reward. For example, a child says drink and is rewarded by a drink. Chomky's grammarian theory (1957, 1965) suggests the grammar of language is crucial to expressing oneself successfully. This means it is essential to know the correct order of words in a sentence to get a message across, e.g. 'the cat was on the basket', differs in meaning from 'the basket was on the cat'.

These theories gave rise to many language programmes for the practitioner to apply. The practitioner in turn found much of value, but also areas for concern. In particular, the failure of children with severe learning difficulties to generalise and make use of their language learning in other settings.

In the last 20 years this issue has been addressed by two new theoretical approaches, the psycholinguistic and sociolinguistic approaches.

The psycholinguistic theory suggests that language development is built, in part, on cognitive development, i.e. the child's actions and knowledge of the world. Children's words are expressions of what they already know (Bloom & Lahey 1978). For example, a child first learns to communicate his need for more cake by pointing to the cake and later adds the word 'more'.

The sociolinguistic theory of language development emphasises that language is acquired only if the child has a reason to communicate (Harris 1992).

The development of communication described in the scheme of work is based on the functional or sociolinguistic theory of language acquisition. The relationship between communication and cognition is closely observed (see the communication and cognitive framework – Figure 1.1) and relates to the psycholinguistic theory mentioned above.

Examining the sociolinguistic theory in more detail we can see that children acquire communication skills in order to affect the behaviour of others. The emphasis is on the child in a social setting. This social process begins at the earliest pre-verbal level and requires a partner to enable functional communication to develop.

> Early language acquisition ... depends heavily on the use of context by both the mother and the child in forming and interpreting messages. (Bruner 1983: 128)

Coupe O'Kane and Goldbart (1998) describe five fundamental principles underlying this theory.

1. Language is learnt only if the child has a reason to communicate (Harris 1992).
2. Language is first acquired as a more effective means of obtaining things than the child could previously achieve by simpler communication. For example, the child requests a drink by waving a cup at the adult and later learns to say 'drink'.
3. Language is learnt in a dynamic social interaction involving the child and mature language users. This emphasises the importance of positive contacts with linguistically competent people since it is they who provide the input to be decoded and understood. For example, the child learns language not by passively learning a series of words but by leading the adult in play, with the adult supplying the appropriate language for the child's non-verbal communications.
4. As the child matures and produces more complex expressions, linguistic structure is initially acquired through decoding and understanding incoming linguistic stimulation. For example, we are all familiar with the child who runs to get their swimming things when told, 'We will be going swimming later' to which the adult then has to clarify 'no, later'.
5. Children are active participants in the process of learning to communicate, and bring to this learning situation a set of behaviours, both cognitive and social, that allow them to benefit from the adults' facilitating behaviours. While adults play their part in this dynamic interaction the language learner needs certain social and cognitive skills. The adult needs to recognise these skills if the child is to benefit.

This theory has provided us with several important aspects of how the child learns to communicate. The child is an active learner, he requires a partner to supply appropriate linguistic input and this partner needs to be aware of the child's cognitive and social level. Most importantly, the child is motivated to communicate in order to affect our behaviour. The role of the adult as a listener is key.

In the first five years of life normally developing children acquire both understanding of and ability to use spoken language. It is the most complex skill human beings develop.

Whilst we recognise there are potential risks applying findings from normally developing children to children who have severe learning difficulties, such results nevertheless provides us with a sound understanding to support our teaching.

We have divided the development of a child's functional communication into four key stages.

The first stage is from birth to eight months. The new-born baby is not yet able to communicate. When he cries, he is not talking to us, he is reacting to his own physical state, he is hungry, tired or uncomfortable. The role of the adult is to interpret the behaviour and act upon it. This is not easy, but as routines are established, the situation and the time of day all help the adult to interpret more consistently and accurately. As the months go by, the baby reacts to things outside of himself, laughing as the wind blows his hair or as someone smiles at him. The adult responds to most of his behaviours. If he is cross, they try and pacify, if he smiles, they smile back, if he coos, they coo, all the time the adult watches, interprets and responds.

As a result of the adult's continual responses, the child begins to learn he can communicate. For example, every time he repeatedly shouts and looks at the adult he will gain their attention. If he repeatedly pulls the adult to the door they will come. From now on the child learns an increasing range of things he can communicate and clearer ways of doing so.

The first communications are all non-verbal, but nevertheless clear to the adult. He or she may vocalise to gain attention, point to an object he wants, push away his dinner when finished or hand over a bag of crisps to have them opened. The child begins to respond and understand routines and from them, associated key words, 'dinner', 'Daddy', etc.

The second stage begins around the age of nine months. Confidence in communication grows and the range of messages the child can communicate expands. For example, he may wave bye, ask for more, point out things of interest; cars, cows, etc., show things have gone and indicate 'no' most emphatically by shaking his head.

The child uses a unique combination of methods to communicate, for example, pointing to the car and vocalising 'vrmm vrmm'. As before, the adult interprets his communications but now models a better way to communicate. As he points to the car, the adult says 'car'. By supplying the word the child learns both the word and its use in communication. Comprehension develops until the child can understand and act on a variety of words, e.g. 'Find your shoes'.

The third stage begins around the age of two. The number of words used quickly expands and when the child has a vocabulary of 50 to 100 words he begins to join them together. These are not

*Development of functional language*

9

grammatically correct sentences, but rather a joining of ideas, for example 'bye Daddy', 'more juice'. So persistent and eager is the child to communicate that, with practice, he quickly learns simple phrases and sentences.

The child can use his new linguistic abilities for a range of purposes. He or she can question, 'What that', he can give information, 'New shoes', and he can describe, 'That big cake' and he can certainly direct, 'You go there'. A crucial skill to emerge at this stage is the ability to repair misunderstandings. When a toddler is misunderstood, he does not stand quietly by, he yells his message louder, he takes the adult's hand and shows, he points or he may try another word.

The role of the adult is now changing. They need to model grammatically correct language, answer endless questions, clarify misunderstandings and generally make communication fun and rewarding.

The child's understanding of language is also growing. He can answer basic questions and carry out simple tasks, but always with language related to what is actually happening. Past and future events are difficult for the child to comprehend.

The fourth stage begins at around three years and extends to five. The child's language and experiences grow rapidly. Vocabulary is learnt quickly in all situations, sentences lengthen and become complex, e.g. 'I go to play group with Jenny', 'It's raining I need my boots' to 'I want to draw a picture for Nanny 'cos its her birthday'.

Language is now a tool for learning. Children ask questions to find out information, e.g. 'What does a tractor do?' and 'Where does Nanny live?' Language is used to plan activities 'I gonna make a card for baby then it her birthday then…'. Language can be used to express feelings 'I bored', 'I starving'. They learn to negotiate with variable success, 'You cook dinner then we play'. Language can also be used to find out about words, eg 'I went to Nanny's tomorrow, when is tomorrow, have we had it yet?' Finally language begins to be used creatively, to make up stories and games, and to play with words.

The role of the adult changes again, they are needed to repair confusion, give explanations, provide vocabulary and engage in dialogue with the child.

By the time the average child enters school, they have mastered the basis of language and can use it for a range of functions. They are able to understand language as a medium for learning and use it in their own thinking.

# Chapter 3

# Play and cognition

This brief background is not intended to be a complete discussion of all aspects of play, but to emphasise the important role of play in the development of cognitive and communication skills.

Whatever the level of play, children's favoured activities form the ideal shared activities that will be more likely to motivate them towards better and more successful communication.

The authors follow John and Elizabeth Newson's description of play as a 'Partly random and infinitely flexible opportunity for the extension of, and re-orientation of, the mind and spirit' (Newson & Newson 1979: 11).

The earliest form of play is the discovery of pleasure in exploratory movement and social activity (Ellis 1973). Here the child repeats random movements or vocalisations which give pleasure. Social play, or people play as it can be referred to (Gerard 1986), begins when adults respond to the child's behaviours. The child enjoys the attention and tries strategies to repeat the experience. This leads to the earliest turn taking, when the adult copies the child's behaviour and the child repeats it. These early games may also involve hiding, such as 'peep bo', which develops awareness of object permanence.

Play with objects is at first exploratory, mouthing, hitting, banging, etc. At this stage the child can relate to an object or to an adult, but not both. Later the child learns to share experiences with an adult, such as playing with a toy together, taking turns to hit a drum or watching an event together. In this case the child is relating to both toy or event and adult. The pleasure of a shared experience helps develop the social aspects of communication. Symbolic play skills begin to emerge when the child uses real objects imaginatively, as in pretending to drink from a cup or talking into a telephone. The next stage is the involvement of the adult in this play.

The link between language and cognition is much discussed. Marianne Lowe's work revealed that symbolic play coincides with the emergence of language, especially the aspect of language linked to putting words together. Lowe (1975) and Westby (1980) developed the idea that symbolic (play) skills were essential prerequisites for meaningful communication.

Other studies have successfully demonstrated that teaching cognition can enable children to develop appropriate language skills (Harrison *et al.* 1987). Imaginative play continues to be a key area for language development. Children begin to act out familiar events, clarifying activities and sequences in their minds. This play also allows for endless repetitions of the language used for the chosen event, such as shops, cafes and so on. More imaginative play involving less familiar events develops as the child matures.

All other forms of play give the child the opportunity to use and develop communication skills, whether with peers or adults. For example, construction activity involves planning, while physical play allows the child to experience the meaning of action words.

As children mature, co-operative play with peers allows them to use a variety of language skills such as negotiating, explaining, planning and directing.

## *Drama*

In the English National Curriculum (DfEE/QCA 1999) 'Drama' comes under the section of Speaking and Listening. However, in the Curriculum Guidance for the Foundation Stage (QCA 2000b) it is not seen as a separate subject but as a part of imaginative play.

Drama is an important mode of learning, encouraging children to be active learners. In the developmentally early years, drama can be addressed by offering many opportunities for imaginative play at the appropriate level for the child.

Chapter 4

# Early literacy

This definition of literacy comes from McGee and Richgels (1996).

> Conventional readers and writers read and write in ways that most people in our society recognise as really reading and writing. For example they use a variety of reading strategies, know hundreds of sight words, read texts written in a variety of structures, are aware of audience, monitor their own performances as writers and spell conventionally.

At the Redway School, literacy (reading and writing) is taught in conjunction with the oral communication skills. The purpose of this chapter is to examine briefly the theoretical background to the development of early literacy skills.

According to current research (Burns, Griffin & Snow 1999, Strickland & Morrow 1988, Weaver 1988), children's literacy development begins early in the second year of life with experiences of both oral language and literacy.

According to Johnson and Sulzby (1999), the term 'emergent literacy development' was first introduced by Marie Clay in 1966. Since then a body of research has supported the view of a continuum of learning towards conventional reading and writing. Children acquire literacy skills at different levels at different stages of development. Learning takes place through social interaction with adults and exposure to developmentally appropriate print, e.g. story books (Johnson & Sulzby 1999).

The activities through which children become aware of meaningful print are linked to their cognitive development and oral language skills. This is illustrated by the work of Linda Gibson, a teacher researcher in the USA.

Gibson (1989) observed and defined the early stages of development leading to reading skills in the children she worked with each day in a pre-school setting. She was concerned that very young children were frequently offered formal literacy programmes developed for five- to

*Definition of literacy*

*The development of literacy skills*

six-year-olds, to give them a 'head start'. Her views that literacy is learnt by developmentally young children by engaging in cognitively appropriate activities was reinforced by her experiences. She identified four clear stages which lead to fluent reading and writing.

The first stage of birth to two years is characterised by collaborative games and communication. The same activities which develop language skills support the development of literacy. She noted the importance from about six months of sharing books with a carer. The young child begins to be aware of book-handling skills, engages in naming games with the pictures and most importantly, slowly becomes aware of the symbolic nature of books. The carer and child respond to a non-concrete object – the picture – rather than the manipulation of a toy. By two years old, children begin to process the story into their own form, echoing parts and commenting.

This experience of symbolic representation prepares the child for the next stage, that of Emergent Reader. The emergent reader is aware of a world of print in daily routines, such as shopping lists, calendars, forms, bills and recipes. Print is a means to get things done. In addition, there is a rewarding social network involving print, i.e., the letters and cards between family members. Children become familiar with the significant letter of their own name and later recognise their own name.

At three years old children engage in story telling by talking through their games. Children also explore rhyming patterns which allows them to examine, manipulate and practise the sound patterns of language. This is demonstrated by the pleasure children have in producing and repeating all sorts of chants and rhymes.

At this level of emergent reader, listening to stories is a key activity, but the story teller must use a narrative form which involves talking and helping children make sense of what is read. Children may also enjoy dictating stories at this age.

It is impossible to underrate the significance of this level which precedes independent reading and writing. The teaching style is consistently that of working collaboratively with children.

From four to five years, children become Early Readers. They begin to know the difference between their own writing and drawing and develop a key skill – writing their own name. Children begin to enjoy copying letters in real writing situations and exploring writing patterns. Alphabetic understanding and a love of reading to other people emerge. As children progress, they identify more and more words in a variety of contexts.

Fluent Readers are those who can process print details automatically, handle a variety of print forms and can read at a rate appropriate to the print form.

Gibson notes that horizontal growth – that is, the ability to handle an increasing range of print forms is of equal importance to the vertical growth identified in the four stages.

Nicola Grove (1999) referring to Stackhouse and Wells (1997) identified the skills within four developmental levels. The first level, referred to as Pre-Literate, lists the skills as symbolic representations, speech and language, communication, interest in print and stories and pretend reading and writing. It can be seen that this correlates to Gibson's observations of nought to two-year-olds.

The next level is called Logographic. At this level children recognise whole words. They can use the skills of visual discrimination, auditory discrimination, memory and sequencing and phonological representations. Gibson's Emergent Readers in their world of print would appear to be at this stage.

The third level is the Alphabetic level where children begin to understand letter sound correspondence and develop the skills of phonological awareness and alphabetic knowledge. The Early Readers of Gibson's work are working alphabetically.

The Orthographic level involves the recognition of rules – affixes, suffixes and the use of analogy. The fluent readers in Gibson's work are beginning to deal with print in a variety of ways.

We can use these stages of literacy as a guide to a developmental literacy programme, matching the skills identified by Nicola Grove with the activities observed by Linda Gibson.

## The development of literacy skills and the framework

The descriptions of literacy development by Gibson (1989) and Grove (1999) can be linked to the cognitive developmental levels in The Redway School Curriculum Framework. This gives a framework where the development of literacy skills, cognitive skills and communication skills are shown to be interrelated. See Figure 4.1.

## Goals of literacy

It is important to identify the reasons for learning to read and write as this will influence what is taught and the way in which literacy is taught. The following goals are taken from Rankin *et al.* (1994).

### Aesthetic Goals (concerned with reading and writing for pleasure including stories and poems)

Aesthetic literacy can be defined as enjoyment of language and words. It encourages the examination of, and expression of feelings and ideas. It promotes self-awareness and the development of understanding and empathy with others.

| COGNITIVE SKILLS | LITERACY CONTINUUM |
|---|---|
| Band 1  Integrate people and object play<br>Collaborative play | Shared attention on picture books<br>Intentional communication |
| Band 2  Real objects hold symbolic meaning | Symbolic representation of pictures<br>Naming pictures<br>Echoing parts of story |
| Band 3  Sequences ideas in play<br>Basic concepts of size,<br>colour, number and position | Story telling in play<br>Print in daily routines<br>Social network of print<br>Recognise whole words<br>Important letters, e.g. own name |
| Band 4  Understands abstract ideas,<br>e.g. past and future<br>Early cognitive skills, number<br>alphabet<br>Reasons and predicts | Talk through games<br>Explore sound patterns<br>Know the difference between<br>writing and drawing<br>Letter/sound correspondence<br>Alphabetic knowledge<br>Phonological awareness |
| National Curriculum levels 1–3 | Process a variety of print forms<br>Recognition of rules (analogy,<br>suffixes and affixes) |

Many children with severe and profound learning difficulties will not become fluent readers at an orthographic level at the end of their school careers. However, examining the goals of reading shows that some goals can be achieved by all children.

**Figure 4.1** Framework for the development of cognitive and literacy skills

At its earliest level, aesthetic literacy involves pleasure in language and words, awareness of books and the conventions in their use. The experience of sharing a book can be appreciated from a developmental level of about six months old.

Stories, poems and rhymes can be enjoyed by all pupils. Some pupils take part in sensory stories where a series of sensory experiences are linked by a theme or narrative. Saying and signing chants and rhymes helps children to be aware of words. Other pupils can act out or play with the ideas presented by a story. Story bags provide toys related to a story and help children to understand the sequencing of ideas. Videos of well-known books, together with extracts from the books, help children to appreciate stories which would be too hard to read. For these reasons aesthetic literacy can be part of the literacy programme for all children.

## Functional literacy

Functional literacy combines Survival Goals (these include words and symbols indicating 'danger' or 'poison' for example) with Information Goals (which include reading and writing of lists and simple timetables).

In a society where written information is all around us few would argue that children should leave school unable to access some of this information.

Information and survival goals (functional literacy) frequently involve the recognition of a single word or picture, e.g. 'danger' or 'exit'. Alphabetic skills are not needed to read and understand these essential pieces of information. This means that children who have reached the logographic stage of development are able to achieve this goal of reading.

The reading of symbols (Detheridge & Detheridge 1997) allows children at the logographic stage of reading access to print. However, Grove (1999) examined the evidence and found that the transfer from symbols to print does not happen incidentally. Those children who will progress to alphabetic reading will need to be actively taught.

Children who are nearing the end of their school career need access to a variety of functional literacy skills. The Social Sight Vocabulary may take a priority in their literacy lessons.

Functional literacy not only includes reading but writing. Children need to be aware that writing is an effective form of communication. Functional literacy looks at the reasons for writing, such as simple greeting and messages, lists as personal reminders and the need for a consistent signature.

In the Scheme of Work, children who are assessed at bands two, three and four work towards functional literacy goals.

## Academic or Vocational Goals (defined as reading and writing to support learning and skills)

Academic literacy, or using reading and writing to support learning, involves recording information, making written plans and reading instructions. A level of independent reading and writing is necessary for this goal to be achieved.

The National Literacy Strategy provides a planned programme of study once children have reached the reception year baseline. Before this, pre-literacy activities based on whole word recognition, phonic games, memory games and sequencing skills can prepare children to become active readers and writers. The QCA Foundation curriculum (QCA 2000b) provides guidance and activities for children at this level.

Children at band three who are working towards independent literacy can lay sound foundations by working on the emergent reader activities described by Gibson.

Academic goals can be achieved by children assessed at band three and band four.

The combination of the clear literacy goals combined with a developmental framework is the foundation for the literacy element of the scheme of work.

# Chapter 5

# Using the English scheme of work

The Redway School English Scheme of Work is based on the under-standing that speaking, listening, reading and writing are all communication skills. Speaking and listening (the oral skills) are necessary to the development of the literacy skills.

Children are assessed on communication, cognitive and literacy skills, and placed within one of four developmental bands (all pre-level one of the National Curriculum). The scheme of work links the appropriate communication and literacy functions to cognitive developmental levels.

The scheme of work is devised to allow children to work within one of the four bands. The curriculum framework (Figure 5.1) shows the areas of English to be worked on at each developmental level.

Each band of the English curriculum is in a separate chapter. The main objectives to be taught, the teaching style and the developmental learning style are highlighted in the first page of each booklet. Activities and guidelines to support each of the strands of the curriculum and sample lesson plans follow:

| Band 1 | Band 2 | Band 3 | Band 4 |
|---|---|---|---|
| Communication | Communication | Communication | Communication |
| Aesthetic literacy | Aesthetic literacy | Aesthetic literacy | Aesthetic literacy |
| | Functional literacy | Functional literacy | Functional literacy |
| | | Pre-literacy | National Literacy Scheme |

**Figure 5.1** English curriculum framework

## Aims of the scheme of work

1. To enable teaching of oracy and literacy to take place at developmentally accurate levels for all children.
2. To focus on functional communication in both oracy and literacy.
3. To give access to a wider range of formal literacy skills for the most able children.
4. To give access to aesthetic literacy for all children.
5. To produce a unified scheme linking the four aspects of English, i.e. speaking, listening, reading and writing.

## Planning for teaching the English scheme of work

Local Education Authorities and individual schools require formal planning in different formats. This advice obviously must be adhered to. The aim of this section is to discuss the key elements of planning to teach English to children with severe and profound learning difficulties.

### The purpose of planning

It is possible to identify three main reasons for planning:

1. To achieve balance and coverage of objectives (DfEE 1998).
2. To move towards a long-term goal in a series of stages.
3. To provide a record of work covered during a period of time.

The authors feel that most planning should be concise and informative. It should not be necessary to write long documents or to repeat information.

### Medium-term planning

The objectives in the scheme of work can be identified as medium-term planning objectives. Although each objective may not be achieved within a set number of weeks, in order to ensure that all the objectives are covered, teachers can identify a few objectives to focus on in more detail in each medium-term planning cycle. For example, at band two the communication function of 'action' may become a medium-term objective. This means the teacher devises a series of games and activities where the child is encouraged to use action words such as 'go' and 'stop'. At the end of the period the child will have experienced the use of action words and possibly used them with encouragement. It is quite likely that a child with learning difficulties will not have absorbed the new words into his own vocabulary at the end of such a short period. However he is now in a position to explore further the use of the words in play and communication activities and begin to generalise their use.

All the objectives in each band should be addressed in this manner throughout the school year. In this way, children will experience planned and specific teaching of each of the objectives. Teachers who use the bands to guide all their teaching programmes are in a position to constantly reinforce and generalise the developmentally appropriate language functions. Identifying objectives in this way ensures that all the objectives are covered in the school year.

From our experience at the Redway, it appears that some objectives are truly ongoing. Specifically the literacy skills at the lower bands involve a regular experience with texts and materials. These ongoing objectives can be marked at the beginning of the school year.

Figures 5.2, 5.3, 5.4, 5.5 show a sample of medium-term plans identifying texts and objectives.

| Class: *Primary* | Date: *September–October 2000* | |
|---|---|---|
| **COMMUNICATION** | **AESTHETIC LITERACY** | **TEXTS ETC** |
| **Pre-intentional**<br><br>1. To choose and express likes and dislikes.<br><br>2. Recognition of the familiar – sounds from home. | **Pre-intentional**<br><br>1. To respond to a multi-sensory story. | Sensory story<br>'Time for Bed'<br>  – duvet<br>  – light<br>  – pillow<br>  – toothpaste<br>  – flannel/sponge<br>  – soap.<br>Sounds tape (home sounds). |
| **Intentional**<br><br>Ongoing daily activities<br>1. Greetings<br>2. Drawing attention<br>3. Requesting<br>4. Protesting and rejecting. | **Intentional**<br><br>1. To engage and respond to stories by:<br>  – giving attention<br>  – recalling<br>  – anticipating. | Bag books<br>'Kippers Toy Box'<br>'Can't you sleep Little Bear'<br>'Good Morning PB Bear'. |

**Figure 5.2** English band 1 medium-term objectives

| Class: *Primary* | | Date: *September–October 2000* | |
|---|---|---|---|
| **COMMUNICATION** | **FUNCTIONAL LITERACY** | **AESTHETIC LITERACY** | **TEXTS** |
| 1. To understand and express:<br>– object words associated with home<br>– recurrence (move)<br>– location (home). | 1. To understand pictures represent real objects.<br><br>2. To use object pictures to label the objects. | 1. To respond to a literacy experience by anticipating key events and important phrases.<br>2. Range:<br>– songs and rhymes<br>– story bags<br>– picture books. | As band 1. |

**Figure 5.3**  English band 2 medium-term objectives

| Class: *Primary* | | | Date: *September–October 2000* | |
|---|---|---|---|---|
| **COMMUNICA-TION** | **FUNCTIONAL LITERACY** | **AESTHETIC LITERACY** | **PRE-LITERACY** | **TEXTS** |
| To understand and express:<br>1. Describing:<br>– using colour and size words during home play.<br>2. Questioning:<br>– asking 'what' questions.<br>3. Directing:<br>– direct adult during home and doll play. | 1. To recognise some whole words and symbols:<br>– class names<br>– symbols relating to topic.<br>2. To use symbols to record information about topic work. | *Range*<br>– rhymes<br>– stories with predictable and patterned structure<br>– stories with a familiar setting. | *Ongoing activities*<br>1. Handwriting.<br>2. Understanding print<br>– tracking text<br>– 1 to 1 correspondence between spoken and written words.<br>3. Phonetic awareness step 1 activities. | As band 1 and band 2<br><br>plus<br><br>'In my Bedroom'<br><br>'Can't You Sleep Little Bear'<br><br>'My First Look at Home'. |

**Figure 5.4**  English band 3 medium-term objectives

| COMMUNICA-TION | FUNCTIONAL LITERACY | AESTHETIC LITERACY | PRE-LITERACY | TEXTS |
|---|---|---|---|---|
| Class: *Primary* | Date: *September–October 2000* | | | |
| To understand and express: <br><br> 1. Directing – direct an adult through a sequence of 2 actions. <br><br> 2. Question – 'Why' – ask 'why' questions. <br><br> 3. Reason To associate reasons and begin to answer challenging questions. | Reading charts. <br> – The daily drinks chart. | To develop critical skills. <br> – why characters do certain actions. | 1. Phonics – step two <br> – continue a rhyming string. <br><br> 2. Word level work <br> – read high frequency words. <br><br> 3. Sentance level <br> – track text left to right, top to bottom. <br><br> 4. Writing <br> – to write in a role play situation. | As Band3 <br><br> plus <br><br> 'It's not fair' <br><br> 'Why Not' <br><br> by Bel Mooney. |

**Figure 5.5** English band 4 medium-term objectives

Class: *Primary*     Date

| | Shared Focus/Text | Band 1 | Band 2 | Band 3 | Band 4 | Plenary | Evaluation |
|---|---|---|---|---|---|---|---|
| **Day 1** | Greetings and News. Teacher to help bands 1–3 to read and share news from home books. Band 4 to tell news | *Communication* • Individual communication sessions – intensive interaction ⓣ | *Communication* • Play in home corner – name household items | *Functional Literacy* • Record news using symbols | *Functional Literacy* • Make a drink chart to use during the week | *B3* To read their news symbols and look at drinks chart and complete it together | |
| **Day 2** | Bands 1 and 2 'Time for Bed' (sensory story) / Bands 3 and 4 'Can't you sleep little Bear' | Continue to explore sensory items | *Communication* • Play bedtime scenes → → – Using 'more' (recurrence) ⓣ | *Functional Literacy* • Record news using symbols – direct adult in play ⓣ | *Literacy* 1. Phonics (step 2) Pebble game 2. Games with high frequency words ⓣ | *B2* To show what they play with. Can they name the objects | |
| **Day 3** | Bands 1 and 2 as above / Bands 3 and 4 as above, 'read' Refrain together | *Communication* • Smelly sessions with soaps and shampoos | *Functional Literacy* 1. Match objects from story to picture 2. Play with objects | *Pre-Literacy* 1. Phonics chants with funny voices 2. *Communication* choice of play activity ⓣ | *Literacy* • Draw a scene from the story. Label with single words or sentences ⓣ | *B4* Read out their sentences. Write up one sentence together | |
| **Day 4** | Bands 1 and 2 as above / Bands 3 and 4 as above, follow story in own copy | *Communication* • Tactile session with hairbrushes and massage brushes | *Communication* Choice of play • Bedroom scenes • Objects from story – using 'more' in play | *Communication/ Literacy* Direct adult to create a large picture of a bedtime scene | 1. *Communication* • Discuss little bear's feelings 2. *Literacy* • Games with high frequency words ⓣ | *B3 and 4* Attempt to retell story to class. Challenge sequence of events | |
| **Ass** | | Do children respond to like and dislike in a consistent way? | To what extent do children indicate 'more' and 'there'? | To what extent do children direct an adult in play? | 1. Which high frequency words are known. 2. Can children retell the sequence of a story? | | |

**Figure 5.6** English weekly planning sheet

## Short-term planning

To achieve the objectives in a planned and consistent manner it is necessary to write short-term plans for each week's work. At the Redway School the literacy hour takes place four times a week. The simple format includes a shared focus session, group work (differentiated by bands) and a plenary. Figure 5.6 shows an example of weekly planning covering the range of objectives from the medium-term plans and associated activities.

The aim of the weekly plans is to show the progression towards the objectives. It is possible to see that each group will be taught by the teacher during the week and that all groups will experience all the aspects of English, i.e. communication, aesthetic literacy, functional literacy and, for the more able children, literacy skills.

There is an important section for noting assessment criteria and a section for an evaluation of the lessons.

## Assessment

Assessment is carried out on two levels. First, teachers or other staff observe and record progress throughout the school year. Ongoing observation of this nature tends to focus on small achievements or changes in communication and literature achievements in different situations.

Second, once a year, a full assessment is carried out on each child. Where it is possible, all those involved with the child are asked for their views. The assessment document attached to the band in which the child has been working is completed. The information from the class record is assimilated and it is possible to see if the child has made true progress towards new skills.

Formal assessments of comprehension skills are part of the process for children in band three or band four but the information should be considered in the light of what is known about the child's effectiveness in communicating.

More advanced children at band four may be making sufficient progress in literacy to benefit from a formal assessment of their skills.

Following the assessment it is possible to set IEP and therapy targets. If the child is making steady progress within a band these targets focus on more effective communication of the language functions from that band. However, if the child is functioning well in his current band then he will progress to the next band. This means he will be working at a more demanding cognitive level in the classroom and towards targets from the higher band.

## *Progression and key stages*

Progression occurs when a child integrates new skills into his learning. In normal development children build on established skills to acquire new ones. For example, a child first learns to show dislike through facial expression, he builds on this to show dislike by shaking his head, then by saying 'no' and then by saying 'I don't like it' and then 'I don't like it because it hurts'.

In the English Scheme of Work, progression is shown in two ways. First, the objectives in each band lead developmentally to the next band. For example, within functional literacy, at band two, children begin to recognise their own written name and, at band three, progress to reading a number of whole words.

Second, and as importantly, children progress by developing a wider range of skills. Taking the example within functional literacy of recognising their own name, progression is also recognising their name as a message (in a card), as a label (on a piece of work) or on a list (on the dinner list).

Consolidating the learning of skills is crucial for the skill to be really learnt and in turn act as the springboard for new learning. Splinter skills learnt and never consolidated disappear all too frequently and do not indicate progression.

The assessment at the end of each band asks for detailed information in each of the objective areas to enable the teacher to see whether the child has made real progress while acknowledging the small steps.

Teaching within the key stages needs to take account of the developmental progression and not to circumvent it. The QCA curriculum guidelines (2000c) support this idea by suggesting at each key stage that children who have not mastered earlier objectives should revisit them. However, to avoid repetition and narrowing of the curriculum, certain texts and set books should be assigned for each key stage. Similarly, in developing communication, older children, who are at the earlier bands of development, can now integrate more experiences into their play. For example, they relate not only to the home corner but also to cafe and shopping experiences.

*Chapter 6*

# The English scheme of work – band one

*Introduction*

A key feature of development at this level is the progress from pre-intentional communication to becoming an intentional communicator. Figure 6.1 shows the objectives for band one. Electronic versions of all these band objectives/assessments can be downloaded from the publishers website: www.fultonpublishers.co.uk.

Developing and responding to children's communication is the major focus of English at band one. Pleasure in books is introduced through aesthetic literacy.

All support to develop communication at this level is child led. The adult's role is to respond, interpret and record the child's communications.

*Learning style – pre-intentional*

Children can:

- engage in sensory activities (visual, auditory, kinaesthetic, tactile, taste, olfactory)
- relate to people or objects but not simultaneously
- explore the sensory properties of objects (mouthing, banging, etc.)
- given time, engage in non-routine activities.

*Learning style – intentional*

Children can:

- integrate people and object play
- explore different aspects of objects (e.g. examine, manipulate, etc.)
- combine objects
- explore the functions of objects.

*Teaching style – pre-intentional*

- Observation and interpretation of the child's responses.
- Use of facial expression, body language and tone of voice by the adult.

- Considered use of approaches to communication (time of day, position, light, noise, etc.).
- Objects of Reference. See page 33.
- Intensive interaction may be appropriate. See page 36.
- Individual time needs to be given to enable the child to engage in an interaction with an adult at their own pace.

## Teaching style – intentional

- Responding to and modelling children's communications. Adults need to consider modelling communication strategies the child will come to learn, e.g. pointing, head nod (yes), head shake (no), waving (greetings).
- Use objects of reference to aid understanding.
- Use of Special time. See page 35.
- Encourage eye contact and turn taking within an interaction.

## General guidelines for children with additional needs

Specific advice for individual children should be sought from the specialist advisors.

### Alternative and Augmentative Communication

Children with physical disability or profound and multiple learning disability will benefit from early use of Alternative and Augmentative Communication.

At the pre-intentional level, switches should be introduced with motivating sensory equipment, e.g. lights, fans, music (tape recorders), vibration toys (footspa), etc.

At the intentional level, single message communication aids such as a Big Mac can be introduced. These can be programmed with band one communication functions, e.g. teacher's name to call for attention.

### Hearing impairment

Children with hearing impairment need their aids in place. Encourage them to use their listening by drawing their attention to environmental sounds, voices, noise-making toys, etc. The adults should confirm that they heard the sound, 'you heard it', and show the source, e.g. telephone. They need to be encouraged to use their voices with confirmation from the adult, 'I heard you'.

| BAND ONE OBJECTIVES |
|---|

## COMMUNICATION

PRE-INTENTIONAL
1. (P1–2) Adults recognise and respond to children's expressions of:
- Likes,
- Dislikes,
- Wants,
- Rejects,
- Recognition of the Familiar and Unfamiliar.

2. (P1) Child engages in interaction using eye contact and turn-taking skills.

INTENTIONAL
1. (P2–3) Children learn to express the following using informal communication systems (e.g. gesture, facial expression etc.):
- Drawing attention,
- Requesting,
- Greeting,
- Protesting and Rejecting,
- Giving,
- Information,
- Responding.

2. Understanding objects of reference and key words associated with routines.

## AESTHETIC LITERACY

PRE-INTENTIONAL
1. (P1–2) To respond to the sensory aspects of a literacy experience (e.g. multi-sensory story/poem).

INTENTIONAL
1. (P2–3) To engage and respond to a literacy experience in the following ways:

- Recall and anticipation,
- Attention,
- Purposeful behaviour.

- Interest and excitement,
- Contrasting moods,
- To promote engagement, enjoyment and motivation.

www.fultonpublishers.co.uk

**Figure 6.1** Band one objectives

### Visual impairment

Children with visual impairment require attention given to lighting. It is important that the light shines on the adult's face and not the child. They need time and encouragement to touch faces and objects as touch will be an important communication channel. Objects of reference are essential for this group and may become their first system of communication. Use and consistency of use of these objects is critical. See Guidelines for Objects of Reference – page 33.

### Autism

Children with autism at band one are particularly vulnerable to confusion and sensory overload. Care needs to be taken with the environment and clear visual communication through objects introduced. Relating to people is a particular difficulty; assigning a key worker to a child with autism can be helpful. Change is usually their most difficult problem and use of their own obsessions can help to deal with this and other difficult situations.

*Communication objectives: band one – pre-intentional communicators*

### 1. Adults recognise and respond to:

*Likes*
Children may indicate like of a person, activity or experience by stilling, smiling, giving eye contact, vocalising or a controlled movement.

*Dislikes*
The ability to communicate negative as well as positive meanings is important. This may mean physically withdrawing, turning away, vocalising, breaking eye contact or agitated movement.

*Wants*
Children may indicate they want a person, activity or action by general body excitement, reaching or by showing an empty drink cup.

*Rejects*
This is usually stronger and more persistent than the negative behaviour indicating dislike.

*Distinguishing between familiar and unfamiliar*
Children may indicate recognition of a familiar person, place or activity by excitement, focused looking, vocalising or relaxing. For example, general excitement on hearing their mother's voice. They

may indicate their awareness of the unfamiliar by distress, tension and unease. Some children may find feeding difficult with a new helper.

## 2. Engage in interaction using eye contact and turn taking:

Pleasure in interaction with others is a key developmental stage. Eye contact and turn taking are two skills which children can use to sustain enjoyable interactions. In addition, control of looking and focusing skills on the objects and people around is part of a growing awareness of the environment.

*Guidelines for communication activities: pre-intentional communicators*

At this level adults are recognising and responding to the very idio-syncratic communications of children. These responses will be related to the situation. For example, Lauren shows she likes the dinner by licking her lips, whereas she indicates she likes music by rocking.

   Children need individual time to develop communication and interaction skills. Consider your approach and greeting. People play and object play should be used separately. Object play should focus on sensory aspects.

## Activities for people play

- familiar rhymes and songs
- familiar touch games, e.g. tickling
- familiar physical routines, e.g. change time, rocking, bouncing, swinging
- peek a boo games
- parachute
- blanket games
- floating cloud game with a colourful scarf
- clapping games
- tapping games
- chasing games

## Activities for object play

When using sensory items, introduce them to the child by offering a choice, pause, allow the child to do something then copy their action, pause for them to repeat and sustain the interaction. Keep copying their actions until they loose interest and then offer another choice.

**Activity list**

- sensory rooms
- activity centres
- materials of varying textures
- sound making toys
- musical instruments
- sand
- water
- pasta
- cornflour
- papers
- finger paints
- dough
- tastes
- smells
- sensory books

*Communication objectives: Band one – intentional communicators*

**1. Children learn to express the following, using informal communication systems (e.g. gesture, facial expression etc.):**

*Draws attention*
Children may begin to demonstrate this early communicative function by vocalising and looking at a person.

*Requests*
Children may make requests by using the adult as a prop – e.g., taking the adult's hand and placing it on a door knob. They may use their developing eye-contact skills to look at the required object and then back to the adult.

*Greets*
Children begin to recognise the social possibilities of communication. At first, they may respond to greetings by smiling, giving eye contact and stilling. As they progress through this stage, children begin to initiate greetings as familiar friends enter the room.

*Protests and rejects*
Children communicate clearly and intentionally that they will not tolerate certain objects or actions, e.g. stiffening and vocalising when they are helped into a coat.

*Gives information*
As the ability to communicate develops, children explore a wider range of subjects. Giving simple information is now developed, e.g. by pointing and showing the adult a new pair of shoes.

*Responds leading to a yes/no response*

The child's responses become more defined. The smile to show 'like' may become a vocalisation and head nod to communicate 'yes'.

*Understanding*

Children begin to understand a number of everyday routines, key words and the associated objects of reference.

Children at this level are exploring their environment and, in particular, exploring the action and function of objects, e.g. scooping with containers, brushing hair with a brush, banging a drum with a baton. Turn taking and involving the adult in their play is established but needs lots of repetition.

As children are at the earliest levels of communication, care needs to be given to approaches and situations that are most conducive to developing communication.

*Guidelines for communication activities: band one – intentional communicators*

## Activity list

- sand and spoons
- rice and containers
- pasta and bowls
- water and pourers
- paint and brushes
- pens and paper
- dough and cutters
- story bags with sensory stories (see page 36 for an example of a sensory story)
- everyday objects: cup, spoon, saucepan, brush, flannel, toothbrush etc.
- dressing up items: shoes, hats, bags, etc.
- balls, hoops, bricks, cars, etc. for turn taking

## Pre-intentional communicators

*Objects of reference*

*Aim of using objects of reference*

To assist in the understanding of what is about to happen.

Children respond to stimuli received and interpreted through the sensory channels, i.e. visual, auditory, smell/taste, tactile and kinaesthetic (movement). This suggests that children are more likely to respond to sensory experiences offered as a 'signal of reference' rather than an object, e.g. the smell of dinner, together with the experience of being fastened into an overall, together with the upheaval in the environment indicate food very clearly.

Children should be given a signal that something is about to happen just before it does. Aim to develop signals which are used frequently and repetitively rather than occasionally (daily, not once a week).

*Signals for pre-intentional children*

- Arrival                Song.
- Drink                  Song and allow child to see and smell.
                         Gently touch mouth with cup or spoon first.
- Lunch                  Song and allow child to see and smell.
                         Gently touch mouth with cup or spoon first.
- Changing               Indicate movement.
- Going outside          Song.
- Home time              Song.
- Quiet time             Burner and blinds down.
- Dark room              Go into room in the light, use fluorescent
                         glove and UV light, gradually darken the
                         room.

## Intentional communicators

*Aim of using objects of reference*

To assist in the understanding of what is about to happen.

Children are actively interested in their environment. Active children will explore objects and try out different behaviours on them including play at using real objects functionally, such as vocalising in a telephone. However, they do not have symbolic understanding. Successful objects of reference are real personal objects such as their own cup to indicate a drink or coat to indicate leaving the classroom.

It is more effective to signal events and activities rather than objects and places. Children are aware of their environment and moving around the school, so an indication of the activities in different rooms could be developed using a key object used in the room, e.g. a book together with an indication of movement to show a story in the library.

As with the pre-intentional children it is important that signals are used regularly and frequently if they are to have meaning.

*Objects of reference for intentional communicators*

Establish areas of the classroom for daily activities:

- Welcome                Area of activities.
- Hello time             Circle of chairs.
- Snack time             Table and chairs.
- Home time              Coats and bags added to circle of chairs.
- Dark room              Fluorescent/spangly glove.
- White room             Novelty torch.
- Soft play              Two coloured balls.

- Swimming        Own costume and towel.
- PE              PE kit.
- Painting/Art    Paintpot and brush.
- Going out       Coat.
- Home time       Bag.
- Singing         Show guitar (or other instrument).
- Toilet          Sponge bag containing personal items.
- Drink           Own cup.
- Lunch           Plate and cutlery.
- Physio          Own aids.

*Special time*

'Special Time' is the name given to communication sessions that are non-directive. It is becoming a commonly used technique to help children with a variety of communication difficulties (Cockerill 1992). It can be used at all four bands by adjusting the adult language and activity accordingly.

The Special Time technique aims to develop all areas of a child's communication. It encourages them to initiate and to realise that they can be an effective communicators. This is done first at a non-verbal level and then by using speech or any augmentative system of communication.

## The special time technique

Special times are stated periods of time during which an adult gives a child her total attention. Cognitively appropriate activities are set up in a designated area. The child is free to do whatever he wishes: to explore the environment, choose an activity and say anything. No attempt is made by the adult to direct the child's activity or conversation. The adult's role is to follow the child and add interested comments either by copying their action or verbally, e.g. 'you are pushing the car' or pushing a car themselves. The key for the adult is to show they are an active and interested 'listener'.

The aim is for the child to eventually take over the commentary for themselves to plan and describe their activity. In these sessions the adult should refrain from making suggestions, directing the child's attention, interfering with play or asking questions.

The sessions have clear beginnings and definite endings. Endings may need to be gradually brought in, e.g. 'soon it will be time to stop'; 'very soon it will be time to stop'; 'when I count to five it will be time to stop'.

This technique is very valuable for children who find it difficult to:
- initiate communication
- make requests/choices
- organise their play/activities.

## Intensive interaction

'Intensive Interaction' is the name given to an approach to communication developed by a group of teachers working with pupils who were experiencing extreme difficulty in learning and relating to others (Nind and Hewett 1994).

Intensive Interaction makes use of the range of interactive games which have been shown to occur in interactions between infants and their primary care givers. The adult attempts to attract and hold the attention of the learner usually by copying one of their actions. Then they attempt to engage the learner in one-to-one interactive games with the emphasis being on pleasure first and foremost. The adult needs to modify their usual language, face and voice to make themselves attractive and interesting to their less able partner.

As well as playfulness, sensitivity is a major theme of Intensive Interaction. It is important for the adult to give a sensitive response to the signals of the child. With more sensitive interpersonal contact the child's behaviours can become readable cues and treated as real communication.

This is an ideal communication technique for band one pre-intentional children.

## Aesthetic literacy – sensory stories

This type of literacy experience can be offered to a small group of pupils. Children begin to respond after they have experienced the story several times. The aim of using a sensory story is to link a series of sensory experiences with a narrative. The narrative should be repetitive and expressive. Nicola Grove and Keith Park in *Odyssey Now* (1996) expands the theme of aesthetic literacy for this group of pupils.

### Example of a sensory story

*The Very Lonely Firefly* **by Eric Carle**

*Objectives*
To be achieved after a period of becoming familiar with the story.

1. To respond to the sensory aspects of a literacy experience (looking).
2. To engage and respond to a literacy experience in the following ways:

### Cognitive focus:
- recall and anticipation (of repeated phrase 'but they were not other fireflies')
- attention
- purposeful behaviour (with switch).

**Affective focus:**
- to promote engagement, enjoyment and motivation.

**Resources**
- torch
- old CDs
- lantern
- fairy lights draped over a black sheet
- paper firefly made from tissue paper and card
- lamp (no shade)
- candle
- sparklers.

*Plan of activities*
1. Darken room.
2. Introduce by looking at the book on its own.
3. Retell using the props at each new page. Take time to introduce each new light and pause between the pages.
4. Line up props in the same sequence as the story.
5. Use switches via switch boxes to activate lights.
   OR
6. Use single torch as the lonely firefly searches around the darkened room.

*Follow on activity*
1. Make sensory book with see through pages to shine a torch through.

## Introduction

Assessing a child's communication at these early stages is crucial; 'it is by being treated as communicators that we become communicators' (Coupe O'Kane *et al.* 1998). At this stage our task is to identify accurately and respond appropriately. Assessment has to be based on observation and discussion with those who know the child best. The following are areas to consider before completing the assessment.

## Observation

Observe the child interacting with someone who knows them well, for example parents, carers or support staff.
- Discuss the interpretation of the child's behaviours.
- Observe the child interacting with a variety of sensory stimuli. To guide your observation, the Affective Communication Assessment (Coupe *et al.* 1998) may be helpful.

- Observe the child interacting with a variety of objects: e.g. do they just stare at it or do they act upon it?
- Observe the child interacting with familiar and unfamiliar people, situations and objects.
- Observe children in situations where it is possible for them to show the negative behaviours of disliking and rejecting.

## Record-keeping

Careful recording of what a child is doing and how it is interpreted is essential in building a clear picture of the individual's communication system. The following may be helpful:

- At these early levels of communicative ability it is important to record not only how the child conveyed something but also your interpretation and the general context in which it occurred.
- All staff should record their observations so that agreement can be reached.
- The Affective Communication Assessment (Coupe *et al.* 1988) can be helpful at this level and provides a record-keeping form that looks at the small and varied ways a child may be communicating.

## Liaison with parents, carers and other staff

To build a comprehensive picture of a child's communicative ability that will lead to a consistent response from those around him requires liaison. In a busy school this is fraught with difficulty but the following suggestions can help:

- Allow staff time to observe and record interaction.
- Allow time for as many as possible to come together to complete the assessment.
- If some key people are unable to attend, a telephone call or questionnaire will enable them to contribute.

## ASSESSMENT: BAND ONE PRE-INTENTIONAL

**NAME**
**D.O.B.**
**DATE**
**COMPLETED BY**


**RESUME**


**ADDITIONAL NEEDS:**
E.g. Hearing Impairment, Visual Impairment, Autistic Spectrum Disorders, Physical Difficulties, Medical/Other Problems

www.fultonpublishers.co.uk

**Figure 6.2** Assessment: band one pre–intentional

---

### PART ONE: COMMUNICATION SKILLS

---

**UNDERSTANDING**
E.g. Understands sensory cue to indicate change

*Comment on the behaviours the pupil uses to convey the following:*

**LIKE**
E.g. By smiling, vocalising, stilling, etc.

**DISLIKE**
E.g. Looking away, withdrawing, changing facial expression, etc.

**WANTS**
E.g. Body excitement, reaching, etc.

**REJECTS**
E.g. By pushing away, crying, etc.

**DISTINGUISHES BETWEEN FAMILIAR AND UNFAMILIAR**
E.g. Shows specific excitement at sight or sound of parent.

*Comment on the following interaction skills:*

**EYE CONTACT**
E.g. Used to sustain interaction or used to focus on an object or activity.

**TURN TAKING**
E.g. Sustains an interaction by vocalising or acting on an object.

    www.fultonpublishers.co.uk

**Figure 6.2** Assessment: band one pre–intentional (continued)

---

### PART TWO: COGNITIVE SKILLS

*Comment on the following cognitive behaviours:*

**SENSORY ACTIVITIES**
E.g. Engages in rocking.

**EXPLORATION OF OBJECTS**
E.g. Mouthing or banging.

**OTHER EXPERIENCES**
E.g. Enjoyed playing in leaves.

---

### PART THREE: PRE-LITERACY SKILLS

**AESTHETIC LITERACY**
*Comment on responses to literacy experiences.*

---

            www.fultonpublishers.co.uk

**Figure 6.2** Assessment: band one pre–intentional (continued)

---

## FUTURE PLANNING

### APPROACH TO COMMUNICATION
Describe the situation, positioning and approach which enables the best interaction.

### TEACHING STYLE
Describe the adults communication, use of objects of reference, etc.

### MAINTAINING CURRENT LEVEL OF COMMUNICATION
Describe the known activities and situations where the child enjoys interaction.

### INDIVIDUAL EDUCATION PLAN TARGETS

---

www.fultonpublishers.co.uk

**Figure 6.2**  Assessment: band one pre–intentional (continued)

**ASSESSMENT: BAND ONE INTENTIONAL**

**NAME**
**D.O.B.**
**DATE**
**COMPLETED BY**


**RESUME**


**ADDITIONAL NEEDS:**
E.g. Hearing Impairment, Visual Impairment, Autistic Spectrum Disorders, Physical Difficulties, Medical/Other Problems

www.fultonpublishers.co.uk

**Figure 6.3** Assessment: band one intentional

---

## PART ONE: COMMUNICATION SKILLS

---

**UNDERSTANDING**
E.g. Understands and responds to object of reference.

*Comment on the way the child communicates the following:*

**DRAWING ATTENTION**
E.g. Vocalising, looking, etc.

**REQUESTING**
E.g. Gestures, taking hand, etc.

**GREETINGS**
E.g. Hugging, waving, etc.

**PROTESTING AND REJECTING**
E.g. Stiffening, throwing, etc.

**GIVING INFORMATION**
E.g. Showing, pointing, etc.

**RESPONDING (LEADING TO YES AND NO)**
E.g. Headshake, head nod.

*Comment on the following interaction skills:*

**EYE CONTACT**
E.g. Sharing attention with an adult.

**TURN TAKING**
E.g. Taking part in physical play such as 'peep bo' or 'round the garden'.

 www.fultonpublishers.co.uk

**Figure 6.3** Assessment: band one intentional (continued)

## PART TWO: COGNITIVE SKILLS

*Comment on the following play behaviours:*

**INTEGRATING PEOPLE AND OBJECT PLAY**
E.g. Rolling a ball.

**EXAMINE PROPERTIES OF OBJECTS**
E.g. Spinning, turning, poking objects.

**PLAY WITH FAMILIAR REAL OBJECTS**
E.g. Telephone, cup, etc.

## PART THREE: PRE-LITERACY SKILLS

**AESTHETIC LITERACY**
*Comment on responses to and engagement in literacy experiences.*

www.fultonpublishers.co.uk

**Figure 6.3** Assessment: band one intentional (continued)

---

**FUTURE PLANNING**

---

**APPROACH TO COMMUNICATION**
Describe the situation, positioning and approach which enables the best interaction.

**TEACHING STYLE**
Describe the adults communication, use of objects of reference, etc.

**MAINTAINING CURRENT LEVEL OF COMMUNICATION**
Describe the known activities and situations where the child enjoys interaction.

**INDIVIDUAL EDUCATION PLAN TARGETS**

---

  www.fultonpublishers.co.uk

**Figure 6.3** Assessment: band one intentional (continued)

# Chapter 7

# The English scheme of work – band two

*Introduction*

Developing communication is the major focus at band two. At this level children are learning through their own activity, linking simple ideas in play with adults supplying the appropriate language for their actions.

It is developmentally appropriate to introduce some functional literacy. The aim at this early level is to gain meaning from simple graphic representations.

The scheme of work has three strands at band two:
- communication
- aesthetic literacy
- functional literacy.

*Learning style*

- Learning takes place through own activity.
- Objects can be combined purposefully.
- Real objects hold symbolic meaning for the child.
- Clear photographs and pictures become meaningful.
- Children begin to sort in play.

*Teaching style*

- modelling by adult
- follow child's lead

At this level language and communication learning is centred on play. Structured play within the classroom setting involves:
- provision of appropriate materials
- provision of appropriate space in which play can develop
- provision of time. This means classroom timetables should allow opportunities for play.

| BAND TWO OBJECTIVES |
| --- |
| **OBJECTIVES** |
| 1. (P4) To understand and express the following meanings:<br><br>• Greetings<br>• Rejection<br>• Action<br>• Location<br>• Disappearance<br>• Object<br>• Existence<br>• Recurrence<br>• Attribute<br>• Non-Existence<br>• Agent<br>• Possession |
| **FUNCTIONAL LITERACY** |
| 1. (P4) To understand that a representation has meaning, e.g. a photograph as an object of reference.<br>2. (P4) To create own representations, e.g. joins in with pretend writing when an adult writes.<br>3. (P4) To use and read graphic representations, such as photographs, pictures, concrete symbols and own written name for the following purposes:<br><br>• messages<br>• labels<br>• captions<br>• records |
| **AESTHETIC LITERACY** |
| 1. (P4) To participate and respond to literacy experiences, e.g. action rhymes<br>2. (P4) To develop an understanding of book conventions, e.g. sharing the contents of a book (the pictures or rhymes) with an adult.<br>3. To experience the following range of literature:<br><br>Action rhymes, short poems, personalised rhymes, story bags, photograph books, texture books, picture books, books with flaps, buzzers, pop ups, etc. |

**Figure 7.1** Band two objectives

Specific advice for individual children should be sought from specialist advisors.

## Alternative and Augmentative Communication

Children who will be slow or unable to develop speech as they emerge from this band will need to have the Alternative and Augmentative Communication developed, e.g. a formal signing system to replace pointing and gesture. Voice Output Communication Aids can be used to express the communication functions from band two.

## Hearing impairment

Children with severe hearing impairment will need their hearing aids in place and a highly visual communication involving sign and clear facial expression within their visual space. As in band one, children need their attention drawn to sound (voice, environmental sound and speech). Children should be encouraged to use their voice at all times.

## Visual impairment

Children with visual impairments will need good light and language supplied by the adult that relates to what they are feeling and hearing. The child can be encouraged to use objects of reference themselves to make requests. See Objects of Reference, page 58.

## Autism

Children with autism will need careful visual explanation of events before they occur. Photographs or simple symbols can be used as cues. Routine use of a 'finished box' helps these children to understand when an activity has finished.

As children enter this band the range of communications that a child can convey grows to include the following. They will not appear in any specific order. It is important that opportunities are given for the full range to be used, first by the adult and later by the child.

*General guidelines for children with additional needs*

*Communication objectives*

1. Children understand and express the following:

## Greetings

Children are encouraged to respond and initiate the greetings 'Hello' and 'Goodbye'.

## Existence

The child acknowledges that an object or event exists. The intention is for the child to show you the object, e.g. the child points to a photo on the wall to draw your attention to it.

## Disappearance

The child comments on, or requests the disappearance of a person/object, e.g. child hands you the plate to indicate their food has gone and they have finished.

## Recurrence

The child requests an item that was there to be given back or repetition of an action that occurred and stopped.

## Possession

The child indicates the relationship between an object or person or an activity and himself, e.g. the adult holds up a coat and the child points to himself to communicate ownership.

## Rejection

The child clearly rejects an action, object or event, e.g. when offered a drink the child turns head away.

## Non-existence

The child indicates that an object does not exist where he expected it to be, e.g. when asked to find his shoes the child turns up his hands and looks puzzled.

## Location

The child comments on the position of an object or person or requests an object to be placed somewhere, e.g. child points to the chair to request you sit beside them.

## Action

The child requests an action such as 'push' when swinging.

## Agent

The child requests a person or an object to carry out an action, e.g. the child hands the adult a bag of crisps for them to open.

## Object

The child names objects or people.

## Attribute

The child comments on the property of an object or person, e.g. child looks at his dirty hands and says 'yuck'.

The activities have been subdivided into exploratory play, physical play and symbolic play.

*Guidelines for communication activities*

| Activities | Communication |
|---|---|
| *Exploratory play*<br>Sand play (wet or dry)<br>Add a selection of scoops<br>and containers | Location, Recurrence,<br>Disappearance,<br>Agent |
| Water play<br>Add bubbles, food colouring,<br>mixes (flour, oatmeal, corn-<br>flakes)<br>Add cups, plates, etc. for<br>pretend washing up. Add<br>clothes for pretend washing | Attributes (wet, yuck),<br>Recurrence,<br>Rejection, Action<br>Early symbolic recognition of<br>objects |

Dough
Add colours, cutters, knife, rolling pins, plates and spoons

Agent, Possession, Attribute, Action

Leaves, pasta, etc.
Add containers and scoops

Disappearance, Attributes, Rejection, Location

Paper
Add colouring pens, glue, sticky shapes, scissors, etc.

Agent (asking for help), Action, Recurrence, Existence

ICT
'Build-up' programmes

Recurrence, Existence, Disappearance

*Physical play*
Movement games
Soft play
Swimming
Ball play
Climbing frame activities
Swinging (in a blanket, on a swing, on a swinging chair etc.)

Action (go/stop), Recurrence, Agent

*Symbolic play*
Children at this level are relating to real items and beginning to use them appropriately.

Use to develop symbolic understanding of self, others and then dolls

Cooking utensils
Tea party equipment

Sponge, toothbrush, hairbrush soap, towel, etc.
Home corner with cooker and pans
Telephones,
Dressing up clothes
Doll's beds and push chairs

This lesson plan is designed for use in a small group.

## Communication – sample lesson plan

### Objective

To express functions of language POSSESSION, AGENT and revise GREETINGS (band one).

### Intended outcome

1. Use greetings spontaneously.
2. Imitates 'possession' or 'agent' meaningfully at an appropriate time

### Teaching points

- offer choice of activity
- comment in simple language on the child's actions
- model communicative functions 'me', 'you' and greetings 'hello' and 'goodbye'
- leave pauses for the child to initiate the interaction.

### Classroom organisation

Groups of more than two children need to have several play activities allowing children to choose freely while the adults move among them.

### Resources

- cars and garage
- telephones, pad of paper and pens

### Lesson plan

1. Allow the child to choose the activity.
2. If he choose phones, model picking up phone or copy if he picks up phone.
3. Model greetings and respond to theirs.
4. Repeat, but this time suggest they choose who answers 'you or me'.
5. Repeat, practising greetings.
6. Extend the activity by modelling taking a message on the note pad.

7. Suggest they choose who takes the next message 'you or me'.
8. Repeat as often as holds interest or move to cars.
9. Warn when the session is to finish.
10. Remove the phones and add 'gone'.

## *Functional literacy objectives*

Functional literacy looks at the reasons for communicating through graphic means. At this early level, it includes mark making. This scheme pre-supposes that children are having extensive experiences of exploring dough, painting materials, drawing materials, sand, etc. There are Information and Communication Technology implications for the physically disabled children. The Occupational Therapist may be able to suggest ideas to enable children to experience mark making.

### Objectives

1. To understand that a representation has meaning.
   This refers to symbolic understanding that one thing can mean another. At this level children can begin to recognise that a picture of a cup which does not look like their own cup still means 'drink'. Some other examples are:
   • The child understands a photograph as an object of reference.
   • The child can recognise a clear drawing or a concrete symbol showing a common object.

1. To create own representations.
   The child intends their marks to have meaning, for example the child wants to write the home school diary with the adult.

2. To use and read photographs, concrete symbols or pictures and eventually their own written name, for the following purposes:
   • Messages, e.g. sticks a picture in the home school book to show parent.
   • Labels, e.g. 'reads' picture labels on drawers to find items.
   • Captions, e.g. sticks own photograph or name on models, artwork, etc.
   • Records, e.g. Making and using photograph books of activities such as records of achievement.

Opportunities should be given to experience the following:
- scribbling independently using pens, crayons and pencils
- drawing with finger in sand, flour, etc.
- using brushes, sponges, etc. with paint
- pretending to write in play
- imitation of adult or peer writing
- seeing symbol, photo or own name labels on common objects in the environment
- fixing own photograph to registration board
- gluing a symbol onto a picture or to label the contents of a drawer
- labelling own creations with name or photo
- signing greetings cards with a kiss or mark
- 'helping' write messages in home school diary
- 'helping' adult to read information such as names on clothes
- making own photograph book
- making a collage of things found on a walk.

*Guidelines for functional literacy activities*

## Objectives

To develop understanding that writing can convey a message.

*Functional literacy – sample lesson plan*

## Intended outcomes

1. To experience mark making for a purpose (writing in celebratory card).
2. To use band two communicative functions during the making of the card.

## Teaching points

- model writing in cards
- key language is the name of the intended recipient
- model band two communication during the making of the card, e.g. 'help?', 'more', 'there'.

## Resources

Materials to make celebratory card.

**Lesson plan**

1. Open a ready prepared card.
2. Make a sample card quickly.
3. Child makes card – offer choice of materials.
4. Model appropriate language.
5. Model writing in sample card.
6. Encourage child to make marks in own card. Interpret it with a note for the recipient.
7. Try to arrange direct experience of giving the card, e.g. allow the child to put it in home bag with a note to parent.

## *Aesthetic literacy objectives*

Aesthetic literacy refers to the pleasure children experience from stories, poems and rhymes. A key feature of aesthetic literacy at this level is the opportunity for an individual or very small group to experience books and stories.

### Objectives

1. To participate and respond to literacy experiences, e.g. action rhymes.
2. To develop an understanding of book conventions, e.g. the need to turn pages.
3. To experience the following range of literature, e.g. action rhymes, short poems, personalised rhymes, bag books, photograph books, texture books, picture books, books with flaps, buzzers, pop-ups etc.

### Activities

## *Guidelines for aesthetic literacy activities*

Opportunities should be given for the following:
- to become familiar with a selection of action rhymes, short poems, songs and books, e.g. joining in with clapping or saying the last word
- to recognise a story/poem by its picture in a book or by the objects associated with it, e.g. choose a book/rhyme or song through gesture, selecting book or by pointing
- to enjoy sharing books and stories with an adult, e.g. listens/attends to signs, turns pages (or signals for help in doing so), lifts flaps, joins in with gestures or vocalisations
- to recognise photographs of family and self. To recognise some pictures and symbols, e.g. make own book of favourite things to share
- to play with items related to favourite stories, e.g. play with items from story bags.

## Objectives

- to enjoy sharing a book with an adult.

## Intended outcomes

1. To have participated in the story by turning pages, lifting flaps and responding.
2. To have experienced the following band two communicative functions – existence ('there') disappearance ('gone') and agent ('you' or 'me').

## Resources

- 'Dear Zoo'
- Several small fluffy toys and a box to hide them in.

## Teaching style

- modelling book conventions (page turning, lifting flaps)
- taking turns with the child
- pace and anticipation
- modelling language.

## Lesson plan

1. Show the book and let the child look through quickly.
2. Read the story through (at an appropriate pace) using tone of voice to encourage interest and anticipation. (NB Without losing pace, encourage the child to lift flaps, turn pages, make animal noises, etc.)
3. Play a hiding game with the animals and box emphasising 'gone' and 'there it is'.

*Aesthetic literacy – sample lesson plan*

## *Objects of reference*

## Aims and purposes of using objects of reference

1. To assist understanding in what is about to happen.
2. To allow the child to relate to out-of-context language and situations.
3. To develop symbolic understanding.

- Children can relate ideas together in their play and in their cognitive development.
- Most importantly, symbolic understanding develops throughout this band. Children can now understand that any cup represents a drink, not just their own cup. It is possible to use representations of events, activities and places.
- As children move through this level they begin to understand photographs, initially of people and places. Simple concrete pictures and symbols can be introduced as children progress through this stage.

## Objectives

*Functional literacy*
1. Understands that a representation has meaning, e.g. a photograph as an object of reference.

*Communication*
1. Uses objects of reference to communicate some meanings at the band two level.
2. Adult uses objects of reference to develop the child's understanding.

## Objects of reference for band two children

Stage 1 – The child uses general objects of reference, not just their own personal ones.
Stage 2 – The objects are attached to a photograph.
Stage 3 – The photograph has a symbol on the back.
Stage 4 – The symbol is used without the photograph.

| | |
|---|---|
| Dark room | Fluorescent glove and photo of room |
| White room | Novelty torch and photo of room |
| Soft play | Two coloured balls and photo of room |
| Swimming | Costume and photo of pool |
| PE | PE Kit and photo of gym, etc. |
| Painting/art | Brush and photo of art |

| | |
|---|---|
| Going out | Coat and photo of playground |
| Home time | Bag and photo of home |
| Singing | Show guitar (or other instrument) and photo |
| Toilet | Sponge bag and photo of room |
| Drink | Cup and photo of cups and drinks |
| Lunch | Plate and photo of dinner |
| Physio | Photo of current physiotherapist |
| Cooking | Wooden spoon and photo of room |
| Bus | Photo of bus |
| Riding | Photo |
| Library | Photo |
| People | Photos |

## Introduction

Assessing progress in communication, functional literacy and aesthetic literacy is crucial to developing progress. Assessing communication continues to rely on careful observation of what the child is communicating and how they do so. Assessing functional and aesthetic literacy requires observations such as the child's understanding of book awareness: book conventions; such as sharing the content of a book, e.g. pictures or rhymes, with an adult.

The following are areas to consider before completing the assessment.

## Observation

Observe the child communicating in different situations.

- A busy classroom is not the best place to observe children communicating to the best of their ability. However it will show the child's level of play and how successful they are at gaining attention and interacting with peers.
- Time should be allowed for the child to play with an adult to demonstrate the highest levels of communication the child can achieve.
- As a child begins to convey a few of the meanings outlined, it may be necessary to set up situations to encourage the use of other meanings.
- Observations at mealtimes and other daily routines will give lots of useful information.
- Observations of free play will often show if a child has truly understood the meanings of representations and book conventions.

*Assessing progress at band two*

### Record-keeping

Children at this level are still fragile communicators and communications will vary from situation to situation. Careful recording of what the child has communicated and how is still essential.

### Liaison

The child's communication exists and develops with many people and in many different situations:
- Support staff should be given time to observe and record interactions.
- Time should be allowed for as many people as possible to complete the assessment, together.

| ASSESSMENT:  BAND TWO |
| --- |

**NAME**
**D.O.B.**
**DATE**
**COMPLETED BY**


**RESUME**


**ADDITIONAL NEEDS**
E.g. Hearing Impairment, Visual Impairment, Autistic Spectrum Disorders, Physical Difficulties, Medical/Other Problems

www.fultonpublishers.co.uk

**Figure 7.2** Assessment: band two

## PART ONE: COMMUNICATION SKILLS

**UNDERSTANDING**
E.g. Objects of reference, key words.

*Comment on the way the child communicates the following:*

**GREETINGS**
E.g. Signs hello.

**EXISTENCE**
E.g. Points to picture on the wall.

**DISAPPEARANCE**
E.g. By word or sign 'bye', 'no' or 'gone'.

**RECURRENCE**
E.g. Repeating part of the action.

**POSSESSION**
E.g. Points to self.

**REJECTION**
E.g. Signing 'no' or shaking head.

**NON-EXISTENCE**
E.g. Shaking head to show that shoes are missing.

**LOCATION**
E.g. Points to a chair for you to sit down.

**ACTION**
E.g. Vocalises to give instructions to start an activity.

**AGENT**
E.g. Uses word or sign to indicate a person to carry out an action.

**OBJECT**
E.g. Names objects by word or sign.

  www.fultonpublishers.co.uk

**Figure 7.2** Assessment: band two (continued)

**ATTRIBUTE**
E.g. Word or sign to say 'yuk'

## PART TWO: COGNITIVE SKILLS

*Comment on the following play activities:*

**PURPOSEFULLY COMBINES OBJECTS**
E.g. Uses shovel to dig sand into bucket.

**USES REAL OBJECTS IN PLAY**
E.g. Uses a brush on own hair, adult's hair and doll's hair.

**SORTS IN PLAY**
E.g. Puts all the cars in the garage.

## PART THREE: PRE-LITERACY SKILLS

*Comment on the following Functional Literacy skills:*

**UNDERSTANDING AND USE OF PHOTOGRAPHS AND/OR CONCRETE SYMBOLS**

**ABILITY TO CREATE OWN REPRESENTATIONS**
E.g. Pretend writing and drawing.

*Comment on the following Aesthetic Literacy skills:*

**RESPONSE TO LITERACY EXPERIENCES**
E.g. Joins in with action rhymes.

**AWARENESS OF BOOKS**
E.g. Points out pictures to adult.

**LIST THE RHYMES, POEMS AND BOOKS WHICH THE CHILD HAS ENJOYED**

   www.fultonpublishers.co.uk

**Figure 7.2** Assessment: band two (continued)

---

## FUTURE PLANNING

**APPROACH TO COMMUNICATION**
Describe the situation, positioning and approach which enables the best interaction.

**TEACHING STYLE**
Describe the adult's communication, use of objects of reference, etc.

**INDIVIDUAL EDUCATION PLAN TARGETS**

    www.fultonpublishers.co.uk

**Figure 7.2** Assessment: band two (continued)

*Chapter 8*

# The English scheme of work – band three

Developing communication continues to be the major focus of English for children assessed at band three. Both language and teaching activities need to be concentrated on the 'here and now' with lots of clear visual clues.

At band three, it is developmentally appropriate to introduce pre-literacy skills in preparation for the more formal literacy skills taught at band four. Pre-literacy at this level focuses on the understanding of whole words and concrete symbols. This is the logographic stage of learning (Grove 1999).

At band three, therefore, the scheme of work has four strands:

- communication
- functional literacy
- aesthetic literacy
- pre-literacy.

*Introduction*

Throughout this band children begin to:
- learn to generalise by repeated opportunities to engage in activities leading to the band three objectives
- sequence ideas in play
- sequence concepts or words in language
- recognise miniatures as representations of larger or real objects
- understand basic concepts and the words which represent them, e.g. colour and size.

*Learning style*

- Relate all concepts and ideas to the here and now or use concrete prompts to aid memory and understanding.
- Use a discursive style, encouraging children to contribute and share ideas.
- Give repeated opportunities on a planned and regular basis to work towards the objectives.

*Teaching style*

As pupils respond to more linguistic input, it becomes important that they can listen.

The pupil's ability to listen continues to develop. It will depend on the complexity of the task and the pupil's motivation. The developmental pattern of listening skills is described as follows (Cooper *et al.* 1978).

### Level 1

Highly distractible. Pupils are constantly distracted by the dominant stimuli.

### Level 2

Engrossed in their own activity and difficult to redirect. Pupils focus for some time on an activity of their choosing. This behaviour is rigid and inflexible and pupils have difficulty tolerating intervention or attempts to modify it by adults.

### Level 3

Can be redirected if touched or name called but not for long. Pupils at this stage are less rigid in their attention. It is still single channelled but often requires the adult to redirect it by saying the pupil's name or 'look'.

### Level 4

Pupils have control of their own attention. Pupils still have single channelled attention but are more able to control it. They look from speaker to task without needing the adult to set their attention.

*General guidelines for children with additional needs*

Specific advice for individual children should be sought from specialist advisors.

**Alternative and Augmentative Communication**

Children who require Alternative and Augmentative Communication need to have their devices available and programmed with the key language functions outlined as communication objectives, so that they can be brought into the English lessons on equal terms with their peers

## BAND THREE OBJECTIVES

### COMMUNICATION

1. P5/6 To understand and express in a formal language system (e.g. speech, sign, VOCA) the following language functions:
   - Socialising
   - Giving Information
   - Describing
   - Questioning
   - Repairing
   - Misunderstandings
   - Directing

### FUNCTIONAL LITERACY

1. READING. P.5 To recognise a number of whole words or symbols, e.g. own name.
2. READING. Recognise and understand the meaning of words/symbols from the social sight vocabulary. (See attached list for band three vocabulary.)
3. WRITING. To understand that writing or symbols can be used for a range of purposes, e.g. Record, Write Messages, Label, Caption, List, Sign Cards and Letters.
4. READING: RANGE. Experience a range of non-fiction texts.

### AESTHETIC LITERACY

1. To become engaged with a story, poem or a video and use it as a stimulus for play or drama.
2. To understand simple story conventions:
   - P.6. title, characters and key events.
   - beginning and ends.
3. RANGE. To experience and respond to the following range of literature:

Modern rhymes and chants     A series of stories
Stories with text and video     Stories and poems with familiar settings
Stories, poems and rhymes with predictable and repetitive structures and patterns.
Stories which relate to the cultural experiences within the group.

### PRE-LITERACY

1. To develop phonological awareness through the step one activities from the National Literacy Strategy Progression in Phonics (DfEE 1999):
   - general sound discrimination
   - speech sound discrimination
   - rhythm and rhyme
   - alliteration.
2. HANDWRITING
   - control pencil to draw lines and circles
   - P.5. Produce meaningful print associated with own name
   - begin to form recognisable letters.
3. READING
   - understand the concept of a word
   - know that information can be retrieved from books and computers
   - know that print carries meaning and in English is read from left to right and from top to bottom.
4. WRITING
   Through shared writing:
   - to understand that writing remains constant and will always say the same thing
   - to distinguish between writing and drawing in books and own work.

     www.fultonpublishers.co.uk

**Figure 8.1** Band three objectives

### Hearing impairment

Children with hearing impairment continue at this band to require:
- to have their aids checked
- to sit near the teacher, or use a radio microphone
- if signing is needed, a member of staff to be allocated as an interpreter.

### Visual impairment

Children with visual impairment need attention given to:
- lighting
- size of visual materials
- clarity of visual materials
- extra time for visual inspection.

### Autism

Children with autism need attention given to the following:
- clear beginnings and endings of tasks and activities
- clear structure to their day
- clear structure to their environment.

Children have difficulties with:
- comprehension of spoken language – may echo spoken language without fully understanding its meaning
- sensitivity to high levels of noise
- visual confusion
- unstructured times of day such as breaks
- unplanned change, e.g. swimming is suddenly cancelled
- group sessions.

## Communication objectives and activities

### Conversational skills

Children at this level need to develop the following social/conversational skills:
- giving and acknowledging greetings and goodbyes
- giving appropriate eye contact
- initiating conversation
- responding to topics introduced by others
- taking conversational turns
- ending conversations.

*Activities:*
- Encourage goodbyes at the appropriate time of day.
- Remind children to look at the speaker.
- Pause during discussions to allow time for children to initiate their own ideas.
- Encourage and remind children to listen to others and then to respond.
- Remind children to keep on topic by saying 'We can talk about that later, now we are talking about...'

## Requesting

Pupils are now requesting through the formal systems of speech, sign or voice output communication aid. However they do require opportunities to practice these skills through verbal choices, e.g. snack time, choice of activity, colours in art, etc.

*Activities:*
- Allow pauses for pupils to initiate requests.
- Develop a culture of expecting signed or verbal choices to be made throughout the day, e.g. snack and drink, work partner, peer to sit next to, colours to use, picture to label, story to hear, play activity, turn.

## Directing

Giving directions or instructions to another adult or pupil means the child has to think clearly in order to convey the message. Opportunities need to be made to enable pupils to give single stage directions, e.g. directing who has the next turn, drink or go.

*Activities:*
- Give opportunities for children to direct classmates or adults, e.g. preparing drinks, next go, take a turn, do the register, do the weather, start the game, give their news, to play the character in a drama.

## Describing

Pupils need to use a range of descriptives including: colour, size (big and small), quality states (good and bad, like and don't like), numbers 1, 2 and 'lots'.

*Activities:*
- Give lots of opportunities for children to offer their opinions, e.g. art (colours, materials, good or bad), maths (numbers), English (listing likes and dislikes).

## Questioning

The language forms of questioning now emerge. The first to encourage are 'who', 'what', 'where'.

*Activities:*
Make a point of modelling questions at every opportunity, e.g. when a visitor walks into the class 'I have a question I need to ask' Who is this?', 'What is your name?' and 'Where do you live?'
- 'What bag?' have a bag of goodies but the children need to ask the question 'What?' to see what is in the bag.
- Have a selection of class photos face down. Pick one up and children have to ask 'Who is it?'
- Use stories that ask the questions 'who?', 'what?' and 'where?'

## Giving information

Children are usually able to give small pieces of information provided they have a visual prompt, e.g. talking about an outing while holding an item connected with the outing.

*Activities:*
- Show and tell at news time.
- Send an item related to an activity home with the child to prompt recall.
- Show an object related to a continuing project to prompt recall.
- Use simple stories to prompt recall of what happened.
- Recap for children, e.g. 'You painted Mum and Dad and we've put it on the wall'.
- Put news on voice output communication aids so the child can tell the news at home.
- Write in the home school book a prompt question for Mum or Dad to ask.

## Repairing misunderstandings

There are two sorts of misunderstandings which occur:
1. The child misunderstands you.
2. You misunderstand the child.

*Activities:*
Misunderstandings will occur frequently while the child is at this early developmental level. You must help the child to recognise that a misunderstanding has occurred and to try the following strategies:
- repeat
- use a sign/symbol
- ask 'show me'
- use another word
- try again later.

## Play

Play for children at band three remains a vital medium for:
- developing ideas
- adults to extend, develop and support the children's language and communication growth
- give a child opportunity to initiate, direct and develop their own ideas in a safe situation.

Play should be set up in the class and the child allowed to move freely between the activities. However, to use this situation to develop the communication objectives adults need to:
- comment on what the child is doing
- give opportunities for the child to initiate, direct and reflect on what is happening
- add to their ideas
- carefully repair all misunderstandings that occur, ensuring that you model how it should have been said.

*Suggested play activities:*
Construction activities
- jigsaws
- making materials: paper, card, sellotape, etc.
- imaginary play, shops, cooking, home corner
- garages
- cars
- train set
- doll play
- dressing-up clothes
- puppets.

## *Communication – sample lesson plan*

### Objective

To experience and express questioning 'who'.

### Intended outcome

To experience questioning.

### Teaching points

- We are so used to questioning children that it can be difficult to give opportunity for them to question.
- Leave space for questioning and try to pick up on confused looks to say 'I think you want to ask the question 'who is it?''.
- Model and slightly exaggerate your own questions.
- Encourage your assistants to put up their hand to ask a question.

### Resources

- set of hats
- screen
- story – 'Knock, Knock Who's There?' (Grindley, S. & Brown, A.).

### Lesson plan

1. Introduce the idea of asking a question.
2. Show symbol and ask aid users and filofax users to find their question pages and symbols.
3. Prompt a support assistant to ask a 'who?' question.
4. Read story of 'who?'
5. Show children the hats and play a game where one by one they go behind the screen, choose a hat and wait for someone to ask them 'Who are you?' Then they come out and show themselves.
6. Finish by recapping modelling: 'John, who were you?'

## *Functional literacy objectives and activities*

### 1. Reading to recognise a number of whole words or symbols

At this level children who are exposed to print will begin to recognise a number of whole words or symbols, beginning with their own name and the names of their peer group. The chosen vocabulary should be short and consist of concrete ideas and words that the children can use in their own functional writing. Reading and writing short sentences can take place at the end of this band.

**Suggested reading vocabulary list**

- names – people at school and home
- favourite activities and interests
- food and snacks
- words which are used daily in school – days, weather, school activities, lunch menu
- Other useful words – To, Like, From, Love, By
- Sentences containing common verbs, e.g. 'I like...', 'I don't like...', 'I went to...', 'Made by...', 'I can'.

## 2. Reading: recognise and understand the meaning of words/symbols from the social sight vocabulary

*Social sight vocabulary – survival vocabulary*
- red – signs in red indicate 'do not' or 'beware'. The response is to stop and wait for your carer to help
- 'Fire exit' – a basic pictogram of a running man
- 'Stairs' – a basic pictogram
- 'Exit'.

*Social sight vocabulary – independance vocabulary*
- Familiarity with the signs in one or two local, frequently visited, public places. For example a cafe might involve reading a picture menu, the 'pay here' or ordering point sign, the toilet signs, the 'litter here' sign.

*Social sight vocabulary – information vocabulary*
- 'Toilet' and the male and female symbols
- 'Enter'
- 'Open'/'Closed'
- favourite things, e.g. snacks, magazines, books, videos, favourite TV programmes.

## 3. Writing: to understand that writing or symbols can be used for a range of purposes

Children should begin to understand that writing is for a purpose such as those suggested in this objective. Most writing activities should focus on using the limited vocabulary suggested for reading above.

*Activities:*

- Record – after an activity, 'I liked the zoo'.
- Write messages – writing short informal notes, e.g. leaving a message on the blackboard to tell the speech therapist that the class is outside.
- Label – name items.
- Caption – a word or sentence to describe own artwork.
- List – shopping or other activity where materials must be gathered together. The aim is to understand that writing can be used as a personal reminder.
- Sign cards and letters – at every opportunity to practice writing own name.

The way children write depends on the development of their physical skills, e.g. sticking whole words or symbols, using a key board, writing over or copying under.

## 4. Reading: range

Children should experience a range of non-fiction texts. These texts should follow the child's interests and contain lots of pictures with simple captions for an adult to read.

*Aesthetic literacy objectives and activities*

## 1. To become engaged with a story, poem or a video and use it as a stimulus for play or drama

This means that the story, poem or video (used alongside a book) engages the child sufficiently that they want to be part of the action. The child may become involved in several ways:

- *Story bags*: Using toys or objects relating to the story to play out parts of the story. After a demonstration of the materials, this is an activity which many children like to develop independently and individually. Adult involvement can include commenting on the child's play (giving a model of language), allowing the child to direct them in the play or lightly structuring the play by giving suggestions to develop a short sequence of events. Some children will co-operate together in their play.
- *Drama*: Children act out part of the story. Most band three children will only become involved in the most dramatic part of the story. A sequence of two or three events is sufficient. Adult involvement includes helping to assign roles, providing a minimum of props, setting the scene and helping children work together. Children can be encouraged to repeat exact phrases from the story (listening and articulation skills), and comment on the characteristics of the people in the story.

- *Choral speaking*: Some pieces of poetry are enjoyable to speak as a group with minimal props and acting out. It is not necessary to understand the whole poem to appreciate the atmosphere, cadences and rhythms.

## 2. To understand simple story conventions

- Title, characters and key events.
- Beginning and ends.
- This concerns the understanding of how stories work and is best taught whenever stories are read. Children should begin to understand the phrases 'beginning' and 'end'.

## 3. Range

To experience and respond to the following range of literature:
- modern rhymes and chants
- a series of stories
- stories with text and video
- stories and poems with familiar settings
- stories, poems and rhymes with predictable and repetitive structures and patterns
- stories which relate to the cultural experiences within the group.

*Pre-literacy objectives and activities*

The *Curriculum Guidance for the Foundation Stage*, published by the DfEE by QCA (2000b) gives developmentally appropriate objectives and activities for band three children in the section 'Communication, Language and Literacy'. This section should be referred to for further objectives and activities.

## 1. Phonological awareness

The activities at step one of the *National Literacy Strategy–Progression in Phonics* (DfEE 1999) are appropriate for this group and should be followed.

## 2. Handwriting

- control pencil to draw lines and circles
- produce meaningful print associated with own name
- begin to form recognisable letters.

The occupational therapist's advice is invaluable for those children with poor upper body control and for those with fine and gross motor difficulties. Some children may need adapted pencils, others may be more effective communicators if they use a keyboard.

*Activities*
- Provide lots of opportunity to use hand control to play with dough, pegboards, Duplo, Stickle Bricks, etc.
- Continued use of brushes, pens and pencils to develop and improve fine motor skills.
- Continued free play and structured activities to promote an efficient pencil and brush grip.
- Encourage children to practice letter shapes as they paint, draw and write their names.

## 3. Reading

- understand the concept of a word
- know that information can be retrieved from books and computers
- know that print carries meaning and in English is read from left to right and from top to bottom.

*Activities*
- In whole class or group, pupils work with others to make picture/symbol stories – sequencing left to right, top to bottom.
- 'Read' refrain of a story or poem while teacher or child points to the words appropriately.
- Take a turn to point to words and pictures as the story is read.
- Tell story in own words.
- Make own books with simple words/symbols.

## 4. Writing

Through shared writing:
- to understand that writing remains constant and will always say the same thing
- to distinguish between writing and drawing in books and in own work.

*Activities*
- In whole class or small group sessions, pupils share with adult a range of books and talk about the purpose of writing/drawing.
- Make whole-class book in which pupils draw and teacher

writes the caption. Use of whole-class discussion to point out the meaning of both.

- Develop individual news picture books in which pupils begin to write captions.
- Model writing including simple sentences and punctuation.

## Objectives

1. Communication – to give information.
2. Communication – to give directions.
3. Functional literacy – use words/symbols to write a list.
4. Pre-literacy – to track text top to bottom.

## Intended outcomes

1. To take part in the shared writing of the shopping list.
2. To understand the purpose of writing a list as a reminder for a shopping excursion.

## Resources

1. Either a picture of the item to be cooked or some cookery utensils.
2. Large paper or white board and pens.
3. Prepared symbols of key items for sandwiches (bread, butter) or draw them directly onto the paper/white board.

## Teaching style

1. Use prompts to remind children of the purpose of the list – a picture of the finished product, e.g. some sandwiches.
2. Minimise direct questioning, try inviting pupils to elaborate, make suggestions, clarify their ideas, echo what they have said or give non-verbal invitations.
3. Use signing.

## Lesson plan

*Shared writing*
1. Show prompt (utensils or picture) and explain that it is cookery today and the ingredients need to be bought.
2. Write 'shopping list' and add a picture or symbol of the sandwiches on the paper and ask for suggestions.

3. Refer each suggestion to the group as a whole. Encourage members of the group to direct you to write up their own ideas for sandwich fillings. Add or draw a symbol if possible. Discuss how many fillings it is practical to buy.
4. Ask child to point, while group read through the list.

*Activity*
1. While the list is copied onto smaller paper, group prepare to go to the shop (coats, bags, money).
2. Members of the group are encouraged to refer to the list in the shop.

*Plenary*
1. On return to school, compare ingredients with the original list.

*Literacy – sample lesson plan no. 2*

**Objectives**

1. Communication – to understand and use the descriptive terms 'small' and the colour words.
2. Communication – to question 'what'.
3. Aesthetic literacy – to experience poems with repetitive structures and patterns.
4. Pre-literacy – to track text in the right order and to make one-to-one correspondence between written words and spoken words.

**Outcomes**

1. To have taken part in the shared reading of the text.
2. To use the question 'What?' and some colour words appropriately.

**Resources**

1. 'In the Small Small Pond' by Denise Fleming.
2. Cut-outs of frogs, geese, bugs, tadpoles and dragonflies, colouring pens, glue, pond outlines.

**Teaching style**

1. Assuming a group of two to three children, sit centrally to ensure everyone can see and touch the book. Encourage children to point to words as you read, turn the pages and question.
2. Use of role reversal where each child has a chance to be the teacher and question the others.
3. Model reading and asking of simple questions.

**Lesson plan**

*Shared reading*
1. Read the story emphasising the rhymes, linger over each page pointing out the colours in the pictures.
2. Flip through the book to find favourite pages. Say the rhymes together, clapping rhythms.
3. Demonstrate how to make a picture of the pond.

*Activity*
1. Children stick and colour to make their own pictures of the pond. Pens are kept by the teacher and must be requested by colour.

*Plenary*
Look at everyone's pictures. Children ask each other 'what?' and listen to description of colours in each picture.

## Story bags

A story bag is a book with a range of props to illustrate the story contained in a bag.

**Using a story bag**

Before you start:
1. Take time to get to know the story and the props really well.
2. If you are telling the story to more than two children you will need to find additional props so that everyone can play.

Reading the story
1. Look through the book quickly with the children, pointing out the most important features, for example 'This is a story about a rainbow fish, there he is... and there'.
2. Look at the props together and identify them.
3. Read the story using the props to illustrate the story. Then allow the children to play with the props.

*Or* read the story without the props and then encourage the children to play the story using the props. *Or* read the story while the children hold the props.
4. You can also:
   Use the props to retell a story.
   Make up a new ending or develop the story further using the props to stimulate ideas.
5. Demonstrate how to play with the props then give the children lots of opportunities to play themselves.

*Assessing progress at band three*

## Introduction

Assessing progress at band three is divided into two key areas:
- communication
- literacy skills

At band three children are now using some formal system of communication: speech, sign or voice output communication aid, together with a range of informal gestures. Assessing progress continues to depend on careful observation together with use of familiar standardised assessment.

## Observation

Assessment requires careful observation of the child. Situations vary and will affect the child's ability to communicate. It is important to distinguish between the following types of situation:
- the child communicating only with adult prompts
- the child in a situation not conducive to communication, e.g. parallel play with a silent partner
- the child is relaxed with family or close friend
- the child is relaxed with an adult as an 'active listener'. This demonstrates the highest level of communication that the child is currently achieving.

## Record keeping

It is suggested that records be kept over the year of samples of the child's utterances and communications. It is important to try and note the methods of communications used, e.g. 'Me' (speech), 'go' (sign), 'Nannie's' (VOCA), 'soon' (points to the calendar).

## Liaison

Children at band three are still at the early stages of communication development. Parents and carers continue to be key contributors to the assessment and follow-up plans. Discussion continues to be important before completing the assessment.

## Formal assessment

Formal assessment of a child's understanding and expression can also assist with planning. Speech and language therapists can offer such assessment or use can be made of a range of tests, such as:

- *Derbyshire Language Scheme Assessment* (Knowles & Masidlover 1982)
- *Reynell Language Scales* (Reynell & Huntly 1987)

## Literacy skills

Emerging literacy skills develop in a meaningful context, e.g. child signs a card to send to their granny. Assessment is through observation of children in different situations and commenting under the headings.

## ASSESSMENT:  BAND THREE

**NAME**
**D.O.B.**
**DATE**
**COMPLETED BY**


**RESUME**


**ADDITIONAL NEEDS:**
E.g. Hearing Impairment, Visual Impairment, Autistic Spectrum Disorders, Physical Difficulties,
Medical/Other Problems

www.fultonpublishers.co.uk

**Figure 8.2**  Assessment: band three

---

**PART ONE: COMMUNICATION SKILLS**

---

**LISTENING/ATTENTION SKILLS**


**UNDERSTANDING**
Results of a formal test.


*Comment on the ways the child expresses the following:*

**CONVERSATION SKILLS**
E.g. Takes conversational turns, responds to topics introduced by others.


**REQUESTS**
E.g. Asks to go on the computer by signing 'computer' and saying 'my turn'.


**GIVES INFORMATION**
E.g. Tells teacher 'Me do PE' on return from gym.


**DESCRIBES**
E.g. Signs 'big cake'.


**DIRECTS**
E.g. Says and signs 'you kick ball'.


**QUESTIONS**
E.g. 'My coat?' or 'What that?'.


**REPAIRS MISUNDERSTANDINGS**
E.g. Repeats, adds a sign or shows a symbol.

www.fultonpublishers.co.uk

**Figure 8.2** Assessment: band three (continued)

---

## PART TWO: COGNITIVE SKILLS

*Comment on the following cognitive skills:*

### SEQUENCES OF IDEAS
E.g. Carried out with imaginative toys such as dolls' houses or garage.

### UNDERSTANDING OF CONCEPTS
E.g. Size, number, colour and position.

---

## PART THREE: LITERACY SKILLS

*Comment on the following Functional Literacy skills:*

### READING WHOLE WORDS OR SYMBOLS
E.g. Knows all the class names and recognises the symbols for the timetable.

### READING – SOCIAL SIGHT VOCABULARY

### WRITING – FOR A PURPOSE
E.g. Signs cards and letters.

### READING RANGE
Comment on the range of information texts the child has experienced.

*Comment on the following Aesthetic Literacy skills:*

### ABILITY TO ENGAGE IN A STORY OR POEM

                        www.fultonpublishers.co.uk

**Figure 8.2** Assessment: band three (continued)

**UNDERSTANDING OF STORY CONVENTIONS**
E.g. Title, characters and key events.


**RANGE OF LITERATURE WHICH THE CHILD HAS ENJOYED**


*Comment on the following Pre-Literacy skills:*

**PHONOLOGICAL AWARENESS**
E.g. Beats words with one or two symbols.


**HANDWRITING**
E.g. Draws people with heads and legs.


**READING**
E.g. Made own book with pictures.


**WRITING**
E.g. Dictates information for the teacher to write in the home school book.

                                         www.fultonpublishers.co.uk

**Figure 8.2** Assessment: band three (continued)

| FUTURE PLANNING |
| :---: |

**TEACHING STYLE**

**USE OF AAC**

AAC systems are used to assist in the development of total communication. Note which systems (sign, symbol or VOCA) are used, who is responsible for their care and upkeep and in which situation they can be used.

**INDIVIDUAL EDUCATION PLAN TARGETS**

  www.fultonpublishers.co.uk

**Figure 8.2** Assessment: band three (continued)

*Chapter 9*

# The English scheme of work – band four

Children who are ready to work within band four of the English curriculum have good basic receptive and expressive language skills. They will be linking their ideas into complex sentences and show an ability to both understand and use verbal reasoning. Most significantly, when children reach this level they are now able to relate to language out of context.

Children can be expected to use their spoken language to enhance their learning through reasoning, questioning and negotiating. The majority of band four children will be ready to work on developing their literacy skills through the National Literacy Scheme. However, older pupils may need to concentrate on the Functional Literacy skills which will serve them effectively when they leave school.

*Introduction*

Language and cognitive functions become interrelated. Children begin to:

- understand abstract ideas and information
- question to find out information
- negotiate with peers
- plan own activities
- reason and predict
- use imagination and fantasy.

*Learning style*

- Plan opportunities for children to use language to develop their understanding, e.g. to ask questions or to work with a peer.
- Use cognitively challenging questions, e.g. 'Why did that happen?', rather than closed questions demanding simple one-word answers.
- Use a discursive teaching style. Try to use the following techniques to elicit communication:

*Teaching style*

- non-verbal invitations
- allow a silence
- clarify ideas and speech
- a personal contribution from own experience
- echo what has been said.

## *Listening and attention*

As pupils respond to more linguistic input, it becomes important that they can listen.

The pupil's ability to listen continues to develop. It will depend on the complexity of the task and the pupil's motivation. The developmental pattern of listening skills is described as follows (Cooper *et al.* 1978):

### Level 1

Highly distractible. Pupils are constantly distracted by the dominant stimuli.

### Level 2

Engrossed in their own activity and difficult to redirect. Pupils focus for some time on an activity of their choosing. This behaviour is rigid and inflexible and pupils have difficulty tolerating intervention or attempts to modify it by adults.

### Level 3

Can be redirected if touched or name called but not for long. Pupils at this stage are less rigid in their attention. It is still single channelled but often requires the adult to redirect it by saying the pupil's name or look.

### Level 4

Pupils have control of their own attention. Pupils still have single channelled attention but are more able to control it. They look from speaker to task without needing the adult to get their attention.

### Level 5

Pupils have now achieved multi-channelled attention. As pupils work, they can assimilate new instructions while continuing their work, e.g. as they are drawing, the adult says 'Add the feet'. The pupil can do so without stopping their work or looking up. This level is considered by Cooper *et al.* (1978) to be essential in order to cope in a mainstream classroom.

| BAND FOUR OBJECTIVES |
|---|

Children should be taught:

### COMMUNICATION

1. To understand and express in a formal language system (e.g. speech, sign, VOCA) the following language functions:
   - Giving and sharing information
   - Describing
   - Directing
   - Questioning
   - Reasoning
   - Predicting
   - Planning
   - Evaluating
   - Negotiating
   - Conversation skills
   - Expressing feelings.

### FUNCTIONAL LITERACY

1. Reading – Follow key icon/instructions on a computer screen. (NB This objective will need to be developed in conjunction with the Information and Communication Technology scheme of work.)
2. Reading – Read print and symbols in the environment. (See attached list for band four social sight vocabulary.)
3. Reading Range – Read text for information, e.g. simple menus, charts, simple recipes, instructions, timetables.
4. Writing – Using handwriting or ICT compose and independently write simple informal letters, messages and lists.
5. Writing – Write/sign name using upper and lower case letters in a consistent style.

### AESTHETIC LITERACY

1. To develop critical skills:
   - to understand and respond to the morals and atmosphere of a plot
   - to relate to characters and their predicaments.

2. To be an active watcher or listener of different forms of media.

3. To use a text or video extract to develop an understanding of:
   - morals
   - atmosphere
   - sequencing
   - reasoning (cause and effect)
   - predicting
   - analysis (are the events in the story fair?)

3. The range of literature should include:
   - stories and poems with familiar settings and those based in fantasy worlds
   - stories plays and poems by significant children's authors
   - retellings of folk or fairy tales
   - literature with patterned or predictable language
   - literature which is challenging in terms of length or vocabulary
   - texts where the use of language benefits from being read aloud and re-read.

### LITERACY

Structured teaching of reading and writing for children assessed at band four will follow the objectives and guidelines of the National Literacy Strategy at the appropriate level.

          www.fultonpublishers.co.uk

**Figure 9.1** Band four objectives

*General guidelines for children with additional needs*

Specific advice for individual children should be sought from specialist advisors.

## Alternative and Augmentative Communication

Children who require Alternative and Augmentative Communication now need access to categories of vocabulary that relate to the curriculum as well as access to language to enable them to use the band four communication functions, e.g. reasoning requires access to words, such as 'why' and 'because'.

## Hearing impairment

Children with hearing impairment continue at this band to require:
- their aids to be checked
- to sit near the teacher, or use a radio microphone
- if signing is needed, a member of staff to be allocated as an interpreter.

## Visual impairment

Children with visual impairment need attention given to:
- lighting
- size of visual materials
- clarity of visual materials
- extra time for visual inspection.

## Autism

Children with autism require attention given to certain areas:
- Their inability to see the whole concept may mean they require constant reminders about the whole topic/subject being taught.
- They may find group work difficult to understand, e.g. speak out of turn or never take their turn, etc. Working through the computer may be less threatening and clearer for them.
- They will continue to require visual explanations.
- They may require personalised timetables to understand the routine of the day.
- They may have excessive literacy/language skills but these mask their total inability to use either meaningfully.

## Giving and sharing information

Children at band three are able to give important key pieces of information that matter personally to them. At band four this develops until children can contribute from their past experiences to the topic under discussion. This needs both encouraging and actively teaching.

## Describing

The concrete descriptions of band three now develop to include the use of descriptive words relating to more subtle qualities of people/objects, e.g. kind or rough. Children can describe situations and events. They should be encouraged to expand their vocabulary of descriptive words.

## Directing

Children now move on from giving single-stage directions, e.g. 'open it', to directing through a sequence of two to three actions to complete a task, e.g. 'Turn the lid, take it out and spread on the paper'. Opportunities need to be given to encourage them to direct in this way.

## Questioning

Children can use more complex questioning 'When', 'Why', 'How' and 'Which'. They should be encouraged to question to find out information related to the topic under discussion. They should be encouraged to use their questioning to acquire new knowledge.

## Reasoning

Children are now able to understand and use verbal reasoning, e.g. 'Mummy is at home because she is not well', and if asked 'Why did the girl get wet?', they can answer, 'Because she went out in the rain'. It is because of this that cognitively challenging questioning from the teacher becomes important.

## Predicting

Children are now able to use their language to predict what may next occur, e.g. when asked 'What will happen if we heat the butter?' They will be able to answer 'melt'.

*Communication objectives and activities*

91

## Planning

Children at band four are able to link their ideas in language and now need opportunity to do this in a functional way. They need to be encouraged to plan, e.g. planning what to take to the art room, to the cookery room or on a trip, or planning a sequence of steps to complete a task.

## Evaluating

Children need opportunities to evaluate, e.g. What do they think of their achievement? What would they do next time? Also to be critics of their own work 'That's not right'.

## Negotiating

This use of language is critical to development for a pupil at band four. They need to use language as opposed to physical/behavioural ways to bargain their needs against those of others, to assert themselves and to judge others contributions. This is essential for their own self-advocacy, and how they will be viewed by their peers. It is a difficult language use and is best introduced in concrete ways, such as sharing materials, sharing a task or planning who does what with a partner. The wider self-advocacy issues need to be addressed as they arise and within class discussion. At the Redway, this was addressed when formulating school rules.

## Conversational skills

Conversational skills continue to be important and all the following aspects need to be encouraged and if necessary worked on specifically:
- ability to give appropriate greetings
- ability to vary their style of communication according to a particular person or situation
- ability to take turns
- ability to ensure their contribution relates to the topic
- ability to repair misunderstanding, using Alternative and Augmentative Communication as appropriate
- ability to make appropriate use of: eye contact, physical distance, facial expression gesture, etc.
- ability to understand how and when to interrupt.

## Expressing feelings

At band four, pupils can be encouraged to express their feelings verbally as opposed to behaviourally. This is difficult and is often best addressed in given situations, e.g. 'You're cross because she took your biscuit'.

Group discussions can also be helpful and often form part of the Personal, Health and Social Education curriculum.

As for negotiating, learning to verbalise feelings is best addressed first through the concrete feelings, e.g. hot, cold, hungry, thirsty.

Functional literacy is concerned with literacy for information and survival. Many children learn the social sight vocabulary by recognising the whole words or signs and their meanings. The vocabulary identified in band three should be learnt first before attempting the band four vocabulary.

The ability to read a chart is a key skill, allowing access to information in many different situations. This skill must be actively taught.

*Functional literacy objectives and activities*

### 1. Reading. Follow key icon/instructions on computer screen.

NB This objective will need to be developed in conjunction with the Information and Computer Technology schemes of work)

### 2. Reading. Read print and symbols in the environment.

This vocabulary should be learnt in real-life situations if it is to be meaningful.

*Social sight vocabulary – survival vocabulary*
Vocabulary for Key Stage 4:
1. Red – means stop, read carefully and then act. Some signs are – 'danger', 'no entry', 'keep out', 'hot tap', 'don't cross' (on a Pelican crossing).
2. 'Police' and a police man/woman in uniform.

*Social sight vocabulary – independance vocabulary*
1. Directional arrows.
2. 'Pay here'.
3. 'Push'/'pull'/'press'.
4. 'Hot'/'cold'.
5. 'Wait here'.

6. The signs in several local situations enabling the child to undertake simple shopping trips, e.g. to buy a snack, a magazine and some toothpaste, to visit a cafe and a leisure facility.

*Social sight vocabulary – information vocabulary*
1. Favourite shops and the signs relating to them.
2. Find favourite TV programmes and times.
3. Time telling.
4. Money.

## 3. Reading range.

Read text for information. These activities are best practised regularly in real-life situations.

*Charts*
Charts can be introduced into the classroom, such as a very simple one showing each child's choice of drink for the day. Colouring either the rows or the columns may help children to find their way round a chart.

*Simple menus*
Menus include those with words and pictures in a variety of different food outlets. The school dinner menu is a good place to start.

*Simple recipes*
Easy recipes show the ingredients and utensils needed and list the steps very simply. Some children's recipe books also have pictures or photographs showing the steps in detail. Clear line drawings may be necessary to illustrate utensils or ingredients with unfamiliar words. Children should start by following recipes with one or two steps only.

*Instructions*
Many children love following instructions to create a model or engaging in some other craft. There are lots of examples in activity books of instructions using simple language with attached diagrams. Children can follow instructions of this nature. This is also an opportunity to work with a friend and practice negotiating skills.

*Timetables*
Before reading timetables, children will need lots of practice with simple charts. However, a simple timetable showing a day's activities in school is a good place to start.

## 4. Writing

Using handwriting or ICT, compose and write the following.

*Informal letters*
Informal letters start 'Dear...' and finish with appropriate terms of affection, e.g. 'Dear Nanny,... lots and lots and lots of love and kisses from...'

Children should practice setting out the letter on the page and composing the contents. Children will be more motivated to write to people they actually know. There may be an opportunity to write formal letters in which case correct beginnings and endings should be used and the letter should be set out correctly with date and address.

*Messages*
Messages are short notes written with the intention of conveying information. There are lots of opportunities in schools, e.g. leaving notes to explain where the class has gone for late comers, notes to parents to remind about swimming kit or forthcoming activities.

*Lists*
Writing lists enables children to see for themselves that writing is a useful activity. Lists are written down the page and can be numbered. Lists can be written as reminders for shopping, equipment to take on trips, equipment to collect for an activity, people to invite to a party, games to be played at a party or in PE.

## 5. Writing

Write/sign name using upper and lower case letters in a consistent style. Children should be taught a consistent way to form the letters of their names. Signing names can be practised each day by using a 'signing-in book' as a register.

At band four, children begin to appreciate longer stories. They can recall story events sufficiently to appreciate a story read in chapters each day, or a series of stories with the same characters such as the Kitty stories by Bel Mooney. Children enjoy thinking a little more about abstract concepts such as the motivation of characters and the atmosphere of a particular piece.

*Aesthetic literacy objectives and activities*

## Objectives

1. To develop critical skills:
   - to understand and respond to the morals and atmosphere of a plot
   - to relate to characters and their predicament.
2. To be an active watcher or listener rather than a passive recipient of different forms of media.
3. To use a text or video extract to develop an understanding of:
   - morals
   - atmosphere
   - sequencing
   - reasoning (cause and effect)
   - predicting
   - analysis.

## 4. The range of literature should include:

- stories and poems with familiar settings and those based in fantasy worlds
- stories, plays and poems by significant children's authors
- retellings of folk or fairy tales
- literature with patterned or predictable language
- literature which is challenging in terms of length or vocabulary
- texts where the use of language benefits from being read aloud and re-read.

## Activities

An aesthetic literacy session can be linked to teaching of reading and writing within the literacy hour.

Read a short story or a chapter of a longer story, focusing on key events. Different aspects of the story can be examined on each occasion, e.g. nice and nasty characters, sequencing the events so far, predicting what might happen next.

*Using text extracts*
Extracts from longer pieces of text may be used to enable the children to benefit from more complex pieces of literature. Longer books can be abridged to short chapters outlining the key events. The author's original words should be used.

*Using videos*
The majority of children at the Redway school will use videos and television for entertainment and information. We should aim to develop simple critical techniques to enable our students to benefit fully from these accessible forms of communication.

1. To review a video or book extract, examining:
   • plot
   • character
   • what the child liked about the extract.

2. To use an extract as a focus for speaking and listening skills.
   • morals
   • atmosphere
   • sequencing
   • reasoning (cause and effect)
   • predicting
   • analysis.

3. Give access to more sophisticated or complex texts, e.g. *The Secret Garden*. After watching an extract from the video, a piece of text may have more meaning for the children.

4. Enhance the meaning of a text extract by watching extracts from a good quality video, e.g. watching an extract from *The Witches* (Roald Dahl) will give a sense of atmosphere to the text.

*Notes on using video*
   • Videos must be used judiciously and purposively within a session which allows for the development of oral skills and literacy skills where appropriate.
   • Crucial to the successful inclusion of video is the focus on the child as critic rather than passive recipient.

## *Literacy*

Many children at band four will be able to make progress in alphabetic reading and writing. While some children will continue to recognise whole words and symbols as their main access to literacy, all the children at this level should follow the objectives and guidance from the *Curriculum Guidance for the Foundation Stage* (QCA 2000b) moving on to the early levels of *The National Literacy Strategy* (DfEE 1998 and 1999).

Children can work towards objectives in the following areas.

## *Assessing progress at band four*

### Introduction

To assess children at band four requires assessment of good basic language skills and assessment of a child's progress through the early stages of the National Literacy Scheme.

Assessment continues to be largely through observation but some formal assessments are used.

### Observations

Communication varies in different situations and with different people. Some suggested situations to observe are as follows:

- in a one-to-one situation with a familiar adult
- in a one-to-one with someone less familiar
- in a group situation such as a class lesson
- in a group situation with peers
- in situations that require different language use, e.g. science lends itself to children using planning, reasoning and predicting.

### Formal assessments

There are a number of formal assessments that can be used to assess children's language at this band. The following are examples and they add valuable information

- *Derbyshire Language Scheme* (Knowles & Madislover 1982)
- *South Tyneside Assessment of Syntactic Structures* (STASS) (Armstrong & Ainley 1992).

### Record keeping

It is suggested that records be kept of key utterances the child has used throughout the year. Notes should also be made of other methods of communication attempted. Particular note should be made of unfamiliar situations and how well the child coped and what went wrong if they did not.

Comment should be made under all the headings for literacy together with the results of formal tests.

## ASSESSMENT: BAND FOUR

**NAME**
**D.O.B.**
**DATE**
**COMPLETED BY**


**RESUME**
Include information and some examples about communication methods. Comment on intelligibility.


**ADDITIONAL NEEDS:**
E.g. Hearing Impairment, Visual Impairment, Autistic Spectrum Disorders, Physical Difficulties, Medical/Other Problems

    www.fultonpublishers.co.uk

**Figure 9.2** Assessment: band four

---

### PART ONE: COMMUNICATION AND COGNITIVE SKILLS

**LISTENING/ATTENTION SKILLS**


**UNDERSTANDING**
Results of a formal test.


*Comment on the language system (speech, sign, speech output device) used to express the following:*


**GIVING AND SHARING INFORMATION**
E.g. Discusses own experience in relation to classroom topic.


**DESCRIBING**
E.g. Describing events and use of descriptive vocabulary.


**QUESTIONING**
E.g. Question forms and their use to develop the child's own learning – 'How does that work?'


**REASONING AND PREDICTING**
E.g. If ice melts slowly in the fridge the child can call on their knowledge of the subject to predict it will melt quickly on the radiator.


**PLANNING AND EVALUATING**
E.g. Plans a model by drawing it first. Evaluates completed model by considering how it could be improved.

---

   www.fultonpublishers.co.uk

**Figure 9.2** Assessment: band four (continued)

**NEGOTIATING**
E.g. Working with a partner to complete a task.


**CONVERSATION SKILLS**


**EXPRESSING FEELINGS**
E.g. 'I'm hungry'

## PART TWO - LITERACY SKILLS

*Comment on the following Functional Literacy skills:*

**READING – INFORMATION COMPUTER TECHNOLOGY**
E.g. Understanding of computer icon and instructions


**READING – INFORMATION FROM TEXT**

*Comment and give examples on reading and understanding of charts, recipes, instructions, etc.*


**READING – SOCIAL SIGHT VOCABULARY**


**WRITING – FOR A PURPOSE**
E.g. Letters, messages, lists, etc.


*Comment on the following Aesthetic Literacy skills:*

**CRITICAL SKILLS**
E.g. Discusses how a character feels.

**Figure 9.2** Assessment: band four (continued)

**UNDERSTANDING OF PLOT**
E.g. Sequence of events. Cause and effect.

**RANGE OF LITERATURE WHICH THE CHILD HAS ENJOYED**

*Comment on the work covered and the progress made on the National Literacy Scheme.*
**PHONOLOGICAL AWARENESS**

**WORD RECOGNITION**

**READING COMPREHENSION**
Results of formal assessment.

**HANDWRITING**
E.g. Uses computer or pen.

**WRITING COMPOSITION**

 www.fultonpublishers.co.uk

**Figure 9.2** Assessment: band four (continued)

---

## FUTURE PLANS

**TEACHING STYLE**

**USE OF AAC SYSTEMS**

The system to be used, the person taking responsibility for it and any further training required should be entered here.

**INDIVIDUAL EDUCATION PLAN TARGETS**

---

  www.fultonpublishers.co.uk

**Figure 9.2** Assessment: band four (continued)

*Chapter 10*

# Sharing in success

Our search for an effective partnership between the speech and language therapy service and education began when the school allocated a part-time teaching post to develop language skills. Practicalities dictated that the teacher and the speech and language therapist began to work closely together, initially to avoid professional toe treading and giving out of contrary advice. The teaching post was non-class based, allowing the rapid build-up of a body of knowledge about language development; in return the speech and language therapist developed an understanding of education in the classroom. We were able to attend conferences and in-service training courses together and thus begin to share a body of knowledge related to the environment in which we worked.

At this point we became a very powerful team, able to tackle, with confidence, a range of issues relating to communication development. As a team, we were able to work and plan beyond the narrow boundaries of our own professions.

It was from this position of understanding that we were able to involve our own managers in working together and thus begin to offer a truly integrated service of speech therapy in education.

The development framework is a consequence of this working practice, it aims to facilitate an integrated service by providing a simple shared body of knowledge for teachers and speech and language therapists.

This shared knowledge base, used consistently by both professions at the Redway School, has led to a more productive partnership in addressing educational issues and individual needs.

This chapter describes the challenges we faced, the use of the framework to facilitate integrated working and the effect on staff and pupils.

*Using the framework for effective partnerships between teachers and speech and language therapists*

## Challenges

As we look back to the early days there were three major challenges faced by both professions:
- differing models of service delivery
- differing knowledge of communication development
- time constraints.

## Education

The role of the teacher is to deliver the curriculum to all pupils to ensure their educational entitlement. The teacher tends to focus on language that relates directly to the curriculum. For example the words describing mathematical ideas such as 'bigger' or 'smaller'.

Teachers' knowledge of communication development is varied. Some may have little knowledge while others will have detailed knowledge of certain aspects, e.g. linguistic development if involved with the *Derbyshire Language Scheme* programme (Knowles & Masidlover 1982), or knowledge of early interaction through work with pupils with profound learning disability.

Teachers have an obligation to deliver the National Curriculum. This leads to a full timetable leaving little time for essential learning requirements. It is worth noting that QCA (2000a) seems to have now addressed this issue to some extent.

## Speech and language therapy

Speech and language therapists are both trained and managed by a medical model of service delivery. In this model the aim is to cure or find an acceptable resolution. A cycle of therapy is usually six to eight weeks, it rarely lasts for the child's entire school career.

The speech therapist's job is to develop the child's communication through techniques based on normal child development. In normal child development the child will master language and communication through play and interaction within his environment. This is achieved before entering school to be taught the curriculum through the now understood medium of language. The knowledge of communication development held by the speech therapist is skilled but related to early child development.

Developing communication coherently through the curriculum is a new challenge. Therapists' knowledge of curriculum development is sparse. The need to understand all the curriculum areas is daunting.

Speech and language therapists also have time constraints. Our research (Fraser *et al.* 1998) showed that the allocation of speech and language therapy to pupils with severe learning difficulties is varied. At best it was shown to be one full-time therapist for 50 pupils. Many schools had one therapist for 200 pupils. In these situations the therapist has to devise a working practice which meets the ongoing needs of all the pupils.

Looking at the challenges outlined above, it is not surprising that a resolution has taken years to find or that many therapists leave while the teachers are, as ever, left to struggle on!

The resolution we found is best summarised as follows:

- the shared framework
- shared responsibility for developing children's communication
- integrated working.

The framework is the essential starting point for sharing responsibility for children's communication development. This means both the speech and language therapist and teacher are responsible for developing a child's communication as outlined in the framework. The teacher's role is to focus on and teach functional communication throughout the teaching day. The speech and language therapist's role is to support the teacher through assisting with planning, the delivery of the curriculum, modelling good communication practice in the classroom and joint problem solving.

Sharing responsibility for communication leads to integrated working where recording, assessment, planning and teaching style are common to both professions.

The simplicity of the framework, has enabled all to share the same understanding of communication and development. The division of the framework into just four bands enables teachers to group children by language and cognitive level for many subjects to ensure children can respond at an attainable but challenging level.

While detailed use of the framework does vary from teacher to teacher, all use the broad banding system. This ensures a greater degree of consistent communication teaching and an effective place for the therapist as opposed to the all-too-familiar role as observer or helper.

# Use of the framework

The effect of the speech and language therapist and teacher working from the same framework is the development of a consistent approach to communication throughout the school.

The shared understanding promotes meaningful discussion between staff of the complexities of children's communication difficulties. Sharing the same assessment enables all staff to see the progress as children develop through the bands or learn new skills within a band. Many staff feel more confident in their own communication with the children because they know where the child is and how communication works and develops. They can, rightly, take pride in the fact they have made a major contribution to the child's communication development.

This increased consistency, confidence and enjoyment of communication has enabled children to value their own communication attempts, to be more actively involved in curriculum activities and to know they will, for much of the time, be understood.

# Effect on pupils

The development of communication is valued, not just as a vehicle for teaching the curriculum but as the core of the curriculum. For children with severe and profound learning difficulties this is crucial for their happiness and quality of life as well as their education.

# Bibliography

Armstrong, S. and Ainley, M. (1992) *South Tyneside Assessment of Syntactic Structures (STASS)*. Ponteland: STASS Publications.

Bentley, D. (1990) *Creating a Handwriting Policy*. Reading: Reading and Language Information Centre, University of Reading.

Blischak, D. (1994) 'Phonological awareness: implications for individuals with little or no functional speech', *AAC* **10**, 245–54.

Bloom, L. and Lahey, M. (1978) *Language Development and Language Disorders*. Chichester: Wiley.

Bruner, J. (1975) 'The ontogenesis of speech acts', *Journal of Child Language* **2**, 1–19.

Bruner, J. (1983) *Child's Talk: Learning to use language*. Oxford: Oxford University Press.

Burns, M. S. *et al.* (eds) (1999) *Starting Out Right: A guide to promoting children's reading success*. Washington, DC: National Academy Press. Available online: http://www.napedu /html/sor

Campbell, R. (1982) *Dear Zoo*. London: Puffin Books.

Carle, E. (1995) *The Very Lonely Firefly*. Middlesex: Hamish Hamilton for Penguin Books.

Chomsky, N. (1957) *Syntatctic Structures*. The Hague: Norton.

Chomsky, N. (1965) *Aspects of the Theory of Syntax*. Cambridge, MA: MIT Press.

Clay, Marie (1966) 'Emergent reading behaviour', Unpublished doctoral dissertation, University of Auckland, New Zealand.

Cockerill, H. (1992) *Communication through Play: Non-directive communicative therapy*. London: Cheyne Centre, Chelsea.

Cooper, J. *et al.* (1978) *Helping Language Development*. London: Edward Arnold.

Coupe O'Kane, J. *et al.* (1988) 'Affective communication assessment', in Coupe, J. and Goldbart, J. (eds) *Communication Before Speech*. London: David Fulton Publishers.

Coupe O'Kane, J. and Goldbart, J. (1998) *Communication Before Speech: Development and assessment*. London: David Fulton Publishers.

Detheridge, T. and Detheridge, M. (1997) *Literacy through Symbols*. London: David Fulton Publishers.

DfEE (1998) *The National Literacy Strategy: A framework for teaching*. London: DfEE.

DfEE (1999) *The National Literacy Strategy: Progression in phonics.* London: DfEE.

DfEE/QCA (1999) *English, The National Curriculum for England.* London: DfEE/QCA.

Ellis, M. (1973) *Why People Play.* Englewood Cliffs, NJ: Prentice-Hall.

Flemming, D. (1985) *In the Small, Small Pond.* London: Bodley Head.

Fraser, R. *et al.* (1998) 'A Cinderella service', *Royal College of Speech and Language Therapists, Bulletin* Issue 554, June 1998, pp. 7–8.

Gerard, K. (1986) 'Checklist of communicative competence 0–2 Years'. Unpublished.

Gibson, L. (1989) *Literacy Learning in the Early Years: Through children's eyes.* London: Cassell.

Grindley, S. (1985) *Knock, Knock Who's There.* London: Hamilton

Grove, N. (1998) *Reading for All.* London: David Fulton Publishers.

Grove, N. (1999) *Training Day Materials.* Milton Keynes: The Redway School.

Grove, N. and Park, K. (1996) *Odyssey Now.* London: Jessica Kingsley.

Harris, J. (1992) *Language Experience and Early Development.* Hove: Laurence Erlbaum Associates.

Harrison, J. *et al.* (1987) 'The development of early communication: using developmental literature for selecting communication goals', *Journal of Special Education* **20**, 263–473.

Johnson, D. and Sulzby, E. (1999) 'Critical issue: addressing the literacy needs of emergent and early readers'. [Online]. Available: http:// www.ncrel.org/sdrs/areas/issues/content/cntareas/ reading/li100.htm

Knowles, W. and Masidlover, M. (1982) *Derbyshire Language Scheme.* Derbyshire County Council.

Latham, C. and Miles, A. (1997) *Assessing Communication.* London: David Fulton Publishers.

Lowe, M. (1975) 'Trends in the development of representational play in infants from one to three years – an observational study', *Journal of Child Psychology and Psychiatry* **16**, 33–47.

McGee, L. M., and Richgels, D. J. (1996) *Literacy's beginnings: Supporting young readers and writers,* 2nd edn. Boston: Allyn and Bacon.

Millar, L. (1996) *Towards Reading.* Buckingham: OU Press.

Mooney, B. (1985) *I Don't Want To.* London: Mammoth.

Newson, E. and Newson, J. (1979) *Toys and Playthings.* London: Allan and Unwin.

Nind, M. and Hewett, D. (1994) *Access to Communication.* London: David Fulton Publishers.

Piaget, J. (1952) *The Origins Of Intelligence In Children.* New York: International Universities Press.

QCA (1998) *Supporting the Target-Setting Process: Pupils with special educational needs.* London: DFEE.

QCA (2000a) 'Developing the curriculum to meet the requirements of pupils attaining significantly below age-related expectations'.

[Online]. Available: http:/www.qca.org.uk./overview/age-related.htm

QCA (2000b) *Curriculum Guidance for the Foundation Stage.* London: DfEE.

QCA (2000c) *Draft Curriculum Guidelines for Consultation.* London: DfEE.

Ramsburg, D. (1998) 'Understanding literacy development in young children'. [Online]. Available: http://www.npin.org/ pnews /1998/pnew498/pnew498b.html

Rankin, J. *et al.* (1994) 'Influence of graphic symbol use on reading comprehension', *AAC* **10**, 269–81.

Redfern, A. and Walker, S. (1994) *Helping Children with Handwriting.* Reading and Language Information Centre, University of Reading, Bulmershe Court, Earley, Reading.

Reynell, J. K. and Huntly, M. (1987) *Reynell Language Scales.* Windsor, Berks: NFER Nelson Publishing Company.

Skinner, B. (1957) *Verbal Behaviour.* New York: Appleton-Century-Croft.

Smith, P. and Fidge, L. (1997) *Nelson Handwriting: Teachers Book.* Surrey: Thomas Nelson and Sons.

Stackhouse, J. and Wells, B. (1997) *Children's Speech and Literacy Difficulties: A psycholinguistic framework.* London: Whurr.

Strickland, D. S. and Morrow, L. M., (1988) in Johnson, D. and Sulzby, E. (1999) 'Critical issue: addressing the literacy needs of emergent and early readers'. [Online]. Available: http://www.ncrel.org/ sdrs/areas/issues/content/cntareas/reading/li100.htm

Uzgiris, I. and Hunt, J. McV. (1975) *Assessment in Infancy: Ordinal scales of psychological development.* Urbana IL: University of Illinois Press.

Vygotsky (1962) 'Which came first: language or cognition', in Owens, R.E. (1996) *Language Development: An introduction.* London: Alleyn and Bacon Publishers.

Weaver (1988) in Johnson, D. and Sulzby, E. (1999) *Critical Issue: Addressing the Literacy Needs of Emergent and Early Readers* [Online]. Available: http://www.ncrel.org/sdrs/areas/issues/content/ cntareas/reading/li100.htm

Westby, C. E. (1980) 'Language abilities through play', *Language, Speech and Hearing Services in Schools* **IX**, 154–68.

# Index